DATE DUE

MR 2 5 '99			

DEMCO 38-297

Asian

Americans:

A Study Guide

a
n
d

Sourcebook

Lynn P. Dunn

San Francisco, California

Printed in 1975

by

R and E Research Associates
4843 Mission St., San Francisco 94112
18581 McFarland Ave., Saratoga, CA 95070

Publishers and Distributors of Ethnic Studies
Editor: Adam S. Eterovich
Publisher: Robert D. Reed

Library of Congress Card Catalog Number

74-31620

ISBN

0-88247-304-2

Dedication

To my friend Kim Hai Chun who shared his birthday
and many experiences with me.

Acknowledgments

I am grateful to Glenn Alleman and Michael Juarez, teachers with whom I worked in late fall and early winter of 1970-1971, to construct the Asian American portion of an ethnic studies guide for teachers in Clark County, Nevada, and to Bill Moore and Robert Dunsheath for the support and help they gave that work. From the resulting document, printed in looseleaf form in January of 1971, I have borrowed ideas for inclusion in this book.

I am indebted also to John Cebular, who suggested ideas and research sources as we worked together in the spring of 1971 to improve the Clark County teacher guide, which had been done in so much haste.

Professors J. N. Hook, Alan Purves and Keneth Kinnamon of University of Illinois read draft versions of this book and made suggestions which, so far as I have succeeded in following them, have improved this book in form, proportion and content. Their interest and help have been invaluable.

L. D.

Table of Contents

Introduction

This book is one of a four volume series on American minorities (one volume each on Blacks, Chicanos, Native Americans, and Asian Americans). In each volume three themes are treated: Identity, Conflict, and Integration/Nationalism. Each volume may serve in itself as a text or guide for the student or teacher in the study of a particular minority. The organization of each volume in the same thematic way may lead the reader to important points of comparison or contrast among the four minorities treated in the series.

Though any study of ethnicity in America will probably deal with white racism, it is not the intention here to suggest that Whites have a monopoly on racism or injustice. One may look elsewhere for examples: to the long history of the Jews in many lands and among many peoples; to the persecutions involved in various religious movements; to the Tlaxcaltecas and other Indian tribes who had been subjugated by the Aztecs, and who in turn aided the Spanish invaders in the destruction of their masters; and, more recently, to events in Nigeria, Bangladesh, or in some countries in South America where there have been gross examples of nationalistic chauvinism at the expense of indigenous peoples. No group or society (or even so-called "classless society") seems immune; all humans are potentially victims and persecutors.

These volumes document white racism and some of the problems and struggles minorities have faced (and continue to experience) in the United States. There are other elements of importance which are treated as well: the personal contributions of individuals, and the richness and texture added to American culture by minority groups.

To maintain a sense of objectivity (not that total objectivity is claimed), the practice in writing these volumes has generally been to let events speak for themselves without editorializing. For the sake of objectivity, and to aid the reader in his own search for understanding, sources included for further study quite often represent several viewpoints (some of them bigoted or extremist, on one or more sides of an issue).

Within a given thematic section of each volume, the study outline is basically historical and chronological in development. The aim in each text, though, is to provide the reader a many-dimensioned, cross-disciplinary study experience, with a heavy stress upon humanistic concerns. For example, there is probably more emphasis upon literary sources than upon historical incident or fact in the "Notes and Sources" column of a given volume.

The "Notes and Sources" column provides references to sources which bear upon, and notes which deal with sidelights to--or which expand upon--the parallel "Study Outline." Though most of the sources cited for further study bear directly and importantly upon the study outline, at times a source is given which is merely allusive.

This brief volume is not an exhaustive study, nor does its bibliography contain a complete list of the many publications relevant to Asian American Studies. Rather, this book is intended to serve as a beginning reference text for students and teachers. It should provide a sufficiently broad scope and adequate references for a solid foundation upon which to build. The teacher or student who finds this volume to be a useful tool or text, will, through further study (to which this text may point the way or help the reader find his own direction), discover aspects of Asian American Studies which are not treated here and will find additional important sources for study.

PART ONE: ASIAN AMERICAN IDENTITY

I   Introduction

The primary emphasis of this volume is on Chinese and Japanese immigrants and their descendants in mainland America. Though there are Asian Americans who came from other countries, and though Hawaiian history and culture are strongly influenced by numerous Asian Americans there, such Asian Americans are treated here only incidentally.

Chinese, Japanese, Koreans, Filipinos and other Orientals brought with them to America remembrances of ancient cultures of which they were products. Oriental cultures varied, of course, but there was much to be admired in their rich contributions to world culture: in philosophy and religion; in literature and the arts; in scientific and technological discoveries and inventions; in traditions, habits and social graces of people.

Immigrants from Asia often sought to retain their Oriental identities, their family ties and loyalties. For many years American laws made it difficult to keep up such ties in a way more personal than simple correspondence by mail. These same laws made full identification with America impossible.

There was much in Chinese and Japanese philosophy and tradition that should have made assimilation an easy process. Standards of hard work, frugality and ethics were very similar to those of Anglo-Saxon Protestant America. But white Americans feared the "yellow peril," the stereotype they had created in their own minds. Oriental Americans often played the American game of competitive free enterprise too efficiently or with too great a determination for the comfort of their white neighbors.

Until recently Asian Americans lived in an almost constant identity crisis. They knew that they were Americans with strong loyalties here. But some politicians emphasized their "otherness," using them in unscrupulous hate-campaigns to win votes. Legislation was enacted against Asian Americans, reflecting a narrow chauvanism and prejudice. Despite the odds, Asian Americans distinguished themselves in many ways, to earn a place of respect in America's pluralistic society.

II   Guide and Sourcebook

            Study Outline   *Notes and Sources*

A. Oriental Americans who immigranted to

    America were products of distinguished,

    ancient cultures.

1

Study Outline	*Notes and Sources*
1. Chinese civilization is very ancient, with a record of important contributions to world culture.	(During the Sung Dynasty, 900-1279 A.D., Chinese invented gunpowder, moveable type, the first astronomical clock, and developed inoculation against smallpox.)
a. Chinese were responsible for many discoveries and inventions which led to technological advances. Chinese were probably the first to cast iron. They developed advanced metallurgic and ceramic technologies.	
b. Chinese art, ceramics, painting, sculpture and architecture had gained an eminent place in world esteem long before America became a nation.	Yutang, The Chinese Theory of Art
c. In religion and philosophy, Chinese thought has affected much of the world.	
(1) Taoist teachings stressed detachment, the goal of immortality.	(In Taoist belief, the celestials were legendary characters who attained immortality through transcendance of the temptations of power, wealth and sex.)
(2) Buddhists stressed ideals of philanthropy, good works, and enlightenment.	
(3) Buddhist and Taoist philosophies stressed the need to liberate oneself from all attachments.	

(4) Mencius taught love and sympathy as the basic facts of human life, the newborn baby as the norm of human excellence.

(5) Confucian ideals were loyalty, filial piety, chastity, heroism and selfless friendship; man's primary duty was the use of his talents in the service of his country and family.

(Confucius also taught the doctrine of the mean. Confucian goals were rank, wealth and position.)

d. There were well-developed musical and literary traditions in China. (Chinese literature dated from the 15th Century B.C.)

"The Subtle Thread," in Haslam's Forgotten Pages of American Literature

Buck, Fairy Tales of the Orient

Kao-Tong-Kia, Lute Song

(1) Opera and theatre were presentational in nature (as opposed to the realism of American theatre at the end of the 19th Century and well into the 20th) and were quite "melodramatic" by Western standards.

(2) Women's parts were usually played by men (a custom of the early Grecian and Elizabethan English theatres as well).

Study Outline	Notes and Sources
(3) The Chinese novel has a history as old as that of the English novel; some historical novels include The Romance of the Three Kingdoms, Journey to the West, Dream of the Red Chamber.	Sung, Mountain of Gold (Betty Sung suggests that most Chinese Americans were not familiar with much of the great Chinese literature and philosophy.)
(4) There were also short stories such as "The Pearl-Sewn Shirt."	
(5) Poetry was also a thriving genre. Through the American Poet Ezra Pound, Chinese poetry became an influence on Western literature.	Davis, The Penguin Book of Chinese Verse (The publication of Pound's Cathay in 1915 made Pound, in the words of T. S. Eliot, "the inventor of Chinese poetry for our time." Pound translations are also found in The Classic Confucius and in a number of standard anthologies.)

B. A significant culture developed in Japan.

  1. Distinct Japanese theatrical and literary traditions developed.

    a. Kabuki and Noh theatres provided traditional dramatic fare to Japanese audiences.

    b. Geisha theatre employed women who were highly trained in the social graces and in music and other arts.

Namiki Gohei's "Kanjincho" or Okamuka Shiko's "The Zen Substitute," in Kabuki Plays (might be worth sampling as a classroom reading)

4

c. Japanese literature has a historical   Mishima, The Sound of Waves (a

narrative tradition: Murasaki   modern Japanese novel)

Shikibu wrote The Tales of Genji,

which has been described as the

world's first novel, in 1004.

d. Older Japanese poetry forms included

Tanka (short poems of 31 syllables)

and Choka (long poems).

e. Sokan, who lived in the 15th and   Blyth, Haiku

16th Centuries, is said to have   Faderman and Bradshaw, Speaking

written the first haiku. Basho,   for Ourselves (has haiku by

who wrote in the 17th Century is   Japanese Americans Yone Noguchi

considered the greatest poet of   and Shisei Tsuneishi. Shisei

haiku. Haiku are short (17 syl-   Tsuneishi founded a haiku

lable) poems which present impres-   society in California in 1922.

sions of beauty by joining   This society publishes a

contrasting terms or ideas. Clas-   quarterly devoted to haiku.)

sic haiku often contrast motion and

stillness. William Butler Yeats

(and other Irish poets) and the

American Ezra Pound introduced the

haiku form in their own writings.

In recent years a popular form in

the U.S., haiku poems are found in

the writings of many Americans,

including Wallace Stevens and

Richard Wright.

f. Myths which form the basis of the
    Shinto religion are also an im-
    portant part of traditional
    Japanese literature.

g. Nangwa Bunjingwa (literary)
    painting is an interesting art form
    which combined poetry and painting:
    a poem was written on each painting.

h. There were traditional dance forms
    of several kinds:

    (1) Bugaku or court dances were in-   (There grew to be 160 differ-
        troduced from China and Korea.   ent kinds of Bugaku.)

    (2) Mai, classical dances, are
        characterized by slow, graceful
        motion which calls the whole
        body into play.

    (3) Odori, fast-moving dances, were
        more popular among the masses.

i. There were popular swordsmen or   (In some respects the chivalric
    chivalric hero stories concerned   hero stories are similar to our
    with the restoration of justice   traditional "westerns.")
    and individual heroism on behalf of
    the wronged, and dynastic novels

concerned with the restoration of
order.

2. Japanese culture also provided a
strong sense of identity to Issei, to
Kibei and (in a lesser degree) to
other Nisei.

a. Japanese sculpture was sometimes
massive: some of the Buddha
statues in Japan were engineering
feats as well as works of art.

b. In contrast, Japanese painting had
a delicate quality with a perfec-
tion in design which, like poetry,
caught essential impressions,
leaving out minute details familiar
in realistic art.

Shigetaka, <u>Guide to Japanese</u>
<u>Art</u>

c. Japanese landscape design and
floral art were cultural importa-
tions which gained importance in
America through the influence of
Japanese Americans.

d. Japanese shared some of the religious and philosophical ideas of
the Chinese; though there was by
no means a total identification of

philosophy and religion of the two

countries.

(1) Many were Buddhists; but Shinto,

a Japanese religion, was more

closely associated with Japanese

nationalism.

(2) They did not share the Taoist   (Too, it must be remembered

philosophy, which enabled Chinese   that Japan itself was experi-

Americans to react to mistreat-   encing a strong growth of

ment with passivity; hence,   nationalistic power and im-

Japanese Americans were quicker   perialistic expansion from the

to act against negative experi-   time Japanese immigrants first

ences.   came to America until World War

(3) A number of Japanese immigrants   II. At the same time, China

were converted to Christianity   was experiencing difficulties

before leaving Japan.   at home.)

(4) It was not unusual for an

Oriental to profess an allegiance

to more than one religion--con-

trasting with the either/or atti-

tude of most Christians.

3. Other Oriental countries which have   S. McCune, Korea: Land of

contributed to America's populace had Broken Calm (especially "The

interesting cultures of their own.   Traditional Korean Way of Life"

a. A Korean had invented moveable   and "The Cultural Heritage of

metal type for printing in 1403,   Korea")

Study Outline	*Notes and Sources*

half a century before Gutenberg's
invention, which was the first
major step leading to the vast
expansion of learning and knowledge
throughout the world.

Lee, Anthology of Korean Poetry

b. Koreans had also devised the first
practical system of rain gauges.

E. McCune, The Arts of Korea

c. Despite repeated invasions, Korea
had maintained a strong nationalistic sense of identity, reflected in
its own language (including a
separate alphabet), literature,
dances, music, costume and customs.

d. Thailand, through effective and in-
telligent leadership, was able to
retain its independence when most
Oriental countries, excepting Japan
and China, were made into colonies
in a period of European imperialism.

"New Americans: Where They're
Coming From," U.S. News and
World Report, LXX (June 14,
1971), 12-14. (This article
reveals that many new immigrants are coming to the U.S.
from several Asian countries.)

e. The Philippines has an interesting
cultural background of its own upon
which have been superimposed a
number of outside influences
through commerce or colonization:
Spain's political influence ended

Santos, You Lovely People (Con-
tains stories related to the
Filipino experience in America.)
Rabaya, "I am Curious (Yellow?)"
Robles, "Rapping with One Million
Carabaos in the Dark"; and Vera

with the Spanish-American War, in which U.S. imperialism made the islands an American colony; Arab traders as well as those of other nations had some impact upon the philosophies and customs of Fili- pinos; Chinese businessmen gained a great deal of economic power in the cities. It was not until after World War II that the Philippines gained independence from the U.S.

C. The history of the Oriental American in the United States is a part of his more immediate cultural heritage, and is evidence of his own American identity.

   1. Japanese had been travelers in the New World before the Pilgrims landed in New England.

      a. Carrying survivors of a Spanish shipwreck, a Japanese ship reached Acapulco in August 1610. Some of the Japanese sailors visited Mexico City before returning to Japan.

      b. In 1613, a larger party of Japanese sailed to Acapulco. Some crossed

Cruz, "Sour Grapes: Symbol of Oppression" in Tachiki, Wong, Odo, and Wong's Roots: An Asian American Reader

Faderman and Bradshaw , "Poems: History and the American Dream," Speaking for Ourselves (A good selection of poems written by Asian Americans of many origins.)

Mexico and traveled on to Spain. A dozen Christian Japanese remained in Mexico. (The Jesuit priest St. Francis Xavier had arrived in Japan in 1549 and had converted a number of Japanese.)

2. Other Japanese sailors arrived as a result of storms and ocean currents.

    a. In 1814, three survivors of an Oriental junk were rescued by a British ship off the coast near what is now Santa Barbara, California.

    b. In 1833, swept adrift by a storm, a Japanese sampan loaded with rice made its way across the Pacific and was washed ashore on the British Columbia coast. There were three survivors, who lived for a time with Indians.

3. The Chinese who first arrived did not intend to remain as permanent residents.

    a. Chinese first came as traders, with no desire to remain and settle.

Kaneko, Manjiro, the Man Who Discovered America

Mitchison, The Overseas Chinese (To many, China was the "middle kingdom," the center of the world, with barbarians inhabiting the world outside.

11

Study Outline	*Notes and Sources*

<table>
<tr>
<td></td>
<td>Chinese food, looks, and social customs were the best. The immigrant's usual intent was to return to family and community in China after gaining financial security.)</td>
</tr>
<tr>
<td>b. Several factors influenced Chinese to begin emigrating to America.</td>
<td>Chu and Chu, Passage to the Golden Gate</td>
</tr>
</table>

b. Several factors influenced Chinese to begin emigrating to America.

  (1) The British defeated China in the Opium War, 1839-1842.

  (2) Deterioration of the Manchu Dynasty weakened China's social structure: major rebellions and civil wars resulted; warlords assumed authority; European involvement increased.

  (3) In 1847 three Chinese boys came to the U.S. as students.

  (4) In 1848 three Chinese, two men and a woman, came to the U.S. to work.

  (5) In 1851 there were 25,000 Chinese in California as a result of the discovery of gold.

Notes and Sources (right column):

Chinese food, looks, and social customs were the best. The immigrant's usual intent was to return to family and community in China after gaining financial security.)

Chu and Chu, Passage to the Golden Gate

(See Lyman, "Strangers in the City" in Tachiki, Wong, Odo and Wong's Roots for other details of even earlier Chinese students and workers who were in America before the Opium War.)

Sung, Mountain of Gold (Forty shiploads of Chinese arrived in California in 1850.)

(6) In 1851 Hawaii began importing
Chinese laborers under 5-year
contracts.

(7) In 1864 the need for railroad
workers was apparent; by 1870
there were 63,000 Chinese in the
U.S., with 94% on the West Coast.

4. Demands for cheap labor and the
Chinese Exclusion Act of 1882 led to
Japanese immigration.

a. In 1865 Japanese were brought to
Hawaii on 3-year labor contracts--
without a final clearance from the
Japanese government.

(The Japanese government made
emigration a more difficult
process as a result.)

b. On May 17, 1869, a Japanese immigrant party sailed into San Francisco on board the S.S. China.
Among them were farmers, trades-
men , samurai and four women. They
brought plants and seeds with them
from Japan to plant on land which
they purchased. Their efforts to
start a tea and silk farm were not
successful.

Hosokawa, <u>Nisei: the Quiet
Americans</u>

c. Between 1885, when Japan first
legalized emigration, and 1924 an

Maisel, <u>They All Chose America</u>

13

| _Study Outline_ | _Notes and Sources_ |

estimated 170,000 to 180,000
Japanese came to the Hawaiian
Islands. Strikes and Japanese
governmental policy slowed the
immigration.

   d. After 1885, Japanese immigrants   (There had been 148 Japanese
      began arriving in the U.S.   in the U.S. in 1880.)

   e. In 1889 the first Buddhist churches   (In that same year 2,844 Japa-
      were established in America.   nese entered the U.S.)

   f. In 1900, with annexation of Hawaii,
      12,635 Japanese entered, mostly
      from Hawaii.

   g. In 1905, 12,000 arrived to work
      on railroads.

   h. In 1930, there were 140,000 Japa-   (The largest concentration of
      nese Americans in the U.S.   Japanese was in the Los
                                                      Angeles area.)

   i. In 1960 there were 475,000 Japanese (Of the 475,000 there were
      Americans.   200,000 Hawaiians.)

5. A few Koreans came to America between Shin, "Koreans in America" in
   1902 and 1945. Since then their num- Tachiki, Wong, Odo and Wong's
   bers have grown.   Roots: An Asian American Reader

6. Oriental family patterns and tradi-   Lin Yutang, Chinatown Family (a
   tions influenced the homelife of   novel of first generation
   Asian Americans, but such patterns   Chinese Americans)

and traditions were strongly affected
by American laws and, later, by
American customs.

a. At first, marriages were not
    usually of the western for-love
    type. (Contemporary marriage pat-
    terns are much more like those of
    other Americans.)

b. The Oriental preference for male
    children and the priority of the
    first son were influences in Asian
    American families.

c. Activities, friendship and employ-
    ment were family-centered. When
    discriminatory taxes drove Chinese
    workers out of the gold fields,
    many of them went into business in
    San Francisco; as such businesses
    grew, relatives were given prefer-
    ence in employment. When Japanese
    were pushed out of employment by
    organized labor resistance, they
    too went into business or into
    farming for themselves; again the
    family enterprise was the pattern.

Weiss, "Selective Acculturation
and the Dating Process" in
Tachiki, Wong, Odo and Wong's
Roots: An Asian American
Reader
Lowe, Father and Glorious
Descendant (a biographical
account of a Chinese American
family)
Chuang, Crossings (an impres-
sionistic novel with insights
into Chinese American family
life)
Sone, Nisei Daughter (Japanese
American family biography)

d. Discriminatory laws, which largely

excluded Oriental women, had seri-

ous demoralizing effects upon Asian

Americans for many years.

   (1) Lack of family life created   (Aberrations of behavior which

social distortions in the lives   resulted from these demoralizing

of Chinese immigrants. It is   restrictions became part of the

probable that the widespread   American stereotype.)

gambling, the use of opium and   Lyman, "Strangers in the City"

other abberations were strongly   in Tachiki, Wong, Odo and Wong's

influenced by the lack of stable   Roots: An Asian American Reader

family life such as these men had

known in China. The slave trade

in Chinese girls is directly at-

tributable to the effects of U.S.

laws.

   (2) An 1891 inquiry conducted by   Hosokawa, Nisei: the Quiet

Fujita Yoshiro of the Japanese   Americans (has some of the de-

Consulate in San Francisco, dis-   tails revealed by this inquiry.

closed much gambling and prosti-   This book also presents some

tution among the Japanese in   notable exceptions and shows

America (with an interesting ex-   that such practices changed as

ception in the small Japanese   American conditions changed.)

community at Tacoma). These dis-   (For similar information on

closures are not surprising when   Chinese Americans see also

16

one realizes the effects of U.S. immigration laws. Prior to 1900 the ratio of men to women was 24 to 1; the ratio dropped to 7 to 1 in 1910 and 2 to 1 in 1920. In view of such facts, it is not surprising that among early Japanese immigrants a number of the women were practically forced into prostitution.

Lyman, "Strangers in the City" in Tachiki, Wong, Odo and Wong, Roots: An Asian American Reader.)

(It should also be remembered that marriage between Orientals and Whites was usually prohibited by law.)

(3) Many males looked to other organizations to provide some of the needs which would ordinarily be met in a family: Tongs, the Six Companies and the segregated Chinatowns provided unity and some sense of security to Chinese men.

(See the "Nationalism and Integration" section II B, for details on the Six Companies and the Tongs.)

Lyman, "Strangers in the City" in Tachiki, Wong, Odo and Wong's Roots: An Asian American Reader

(4) A few Chinese scholars, businessmen and professionals were admitted between 1883 and 1943, when most Chinese were not allowed to enter.

(T. V. Soong and Lin Yutang, the scholar and writer, were among the few admitted.)

e. Later generations found chances for normal family life improved.

(Girl babies were born as often as boys to the women who were here.)

Study Outline	*Notes and Sources*

f. Second and third generation Asian Americans concerned themselves with education and with entering the professions. The 1960 census reflected the Asian American stress on the professions and on education. In 1960, 56% of Japanese American males were employed in white collar jobs as compared with 42.1% of Whites; 26.1% were classified as technicians as compared to 12.5% of Whites. (However, the 1959 median income of Japanese American males was a little less than that of their white counterparts.)

Lowe, Father and Glorious Descendant

Sone, Nisei Daughter

Wong, Fifth Chinese Daughter

Lee, Flower Drum Song

Lin Yutang, Chinatown Family

Smith, Second Generation Orientals in America

Median years of schooling completed by different American groups (1960 figures) are as follows:

Japanese	12.2
Chinese	11.1
Whites	11.0
Filipinos	9.2
Negroes	8.6
Indians	8.4

g. World War II and the later Communist takeover of China brought to a halt the practice of sending young men back to the ancestral home for a period of training and education.

Mitchison, The Overseas Chinese

7. With professional training and education to match or surpass any other group, Asian Americans have largely removed themselves from employments

such as their first American for-

bearers found--building railroads;

mining; planting, weeding and har-

vesting crops as hired stoop labor;

or cleaning fish in Alaskan canner-

ies.

8. Their own philosophical and religious

    tolerance and their strongly middle-

    class values made cultural (though

    not racial) assimilation less painful

    for Asian Americans than for some

    other minority groups.   Inada, "Asian Brother, Asian

9. Present-day Asian Americans are in-   Sister" in Takichi, Wong, Odo

    terested in the ancient Oriental cul-   and Wong's Roots: An Asian

    tures which are a part of their   American Reader

    heritage; at the same time they are   Lee, The Chinese in the United

    studying and contributing to   States of America

    America's own culture.   (See also the "Conflict" and

10. Much of the history of Asian Ameri-   "Integration and Nationalism"

    cans that is covered in other sec-   sections of this volume.)

    tions of this volume also relates to   "Uncle Kwok," an excerpt from

    identity: to Asian Americans'   Wong's Fifth Chinese Daughter

    thoughts, feelings, and perceptions   (in Haslam's Forgotten Pages of

    of themselves and to white Americans'   American Literature).

    feelings and beliefs about them.

Study Outline	*Notes and Sources*

D. W.A.S.P. America created its own defi-
nitions of Oriental identity, which
varied from time to time, from group to
group , and which had varying psychological effects on Asian Americans'
perceptions of themselves.

1. There were positive perceptions.

    a. Employers viewed them as profitable
laborers.

        (1) Chinese and Japanese workers had
a strong sense of obligation.

        (2) Newly arrived Asian Americans
were often willing to work at
wages less than Whites were
asking.

        (3) The farming ability of some
Japanese immigrants was excep-
tional.

    b. Much of the Buddhist and Confucian
philosophy, which was reflected
in deportment and in family life,
fit in very well with W.A.S.P.
standards in America.

(The Chinese, who had come
first, had impressed employers
with their willingness to work
without slacking, even without
supervision. And the work
ethic of Japanese is often
compared to that of Puritan
America.)

(Employers in this period of
raw capitalism used Chinese and
Japanese workers as strike
breakers.)

(Falling into the stereotype
trap--thinking that all Japanese
were good farmers--some pros-
pective employers secured a
boatload of immigrants who were
mostly from cities, effectively
bursting the bubble of their own
small myth.)

Study Outline	*Notes and Sources*
(1) Asian American children behaved well, treating parents and authorities with respect.	(Since World War II there is a growing trend for children and wives to act more like their white counterparts.)
(2) What few families there were displayed a solidarity that seemed admirable. Issei parents felt an obligation to sacrifice for their children; and the children, in return, felt a reciprocal obligation.	
(3) The patriarchal family placed the father in the position of authority. But the mothers gave stability to the home.	Chung, "The Trouble with Losing Face is, You Become Invisible" and Ono "Stormy Weather" in Tachiki, Wong, Odo and Wong's
(4) Asian Americans brought with them a tolerance for other beliefs and ideas, which were not matched by other immigrant groups (including Anglo-Saxons) despite Constitutional guarantees.	Roots: An Asian American Reader (These poems explore the feelings and emotional reactions young Asian Americans have toward their parents and to their own roles in American Society.)
(5) Most Orientals brought with them a strong sense of obligation to the community as well as to the family.	

(6) Desires for status and high
    standards of achievement were
    consistent with American ideals,
    though such desires and standards
    often led to conflict.

2. There were negative views of Asian
   Americans' competitiveness: stereotypes were often unfavorable.

a. American labor organizations viewed
    Asian Americans as a threat.

(1) Willingness to work long hours
    for low pay was a threat to the
    security of white workers.

(2) The efficiency of Oriental   History of the Union Pacific
    workers created a demand for   Coal Mines 1868 to 1940
    their services, sometimes at the   (Chapter VI "Chinese Riot and
    expense of jobs for Whites.   Massacre of September 2, 1885.")

(3) Peak demands for labor were often
    followed by slack periods: The
    completion of the transconti-
    nental railroad found great num-
    bers of workers, all of them in
    the West, suddenly unemployed in
    an area where their presence
    glutted the job market. The
    Chinese laborers provided a

handy scapegoat for White unem-
ployment (though, of course, the
Chinese were out of work as
well).

    (4) Immigration (especially of women,
who would serve as breeders) was
opposed.

b. Negative stereotypes developed.

    (1) Betty Lee Sung lists the follow-   Sung, Mountain of Gold
ing as Chinese stereotypes in
America: opium dens, tong wars,
coolie labor, yellow peril, high-
binders, hatchetmen, laundrymen,
waiters, houseboys, slave wages,
unassimilable aliens.

    (2) Japanese (and other Asian Ameri-
cans) inherited a number of the
stereotypes associated with
Chinese.

    (3) Movies and books (and newspapers,   Paik, "A look at the Carica-
of course) exploited the negative   tures of the Asians as Sketched
stereotypes and fears which had   by American Movies," in
been the center of many a   Tachiki, Wong, Odo and Wong's
political campaign: Homer Lea's   Roots: An Asian American
The Valor of Ignorance (1909);   Reader (deals with some older
Hearst International Film   movies and many more recent

23

Service's <u>Patria</u> (1917); <u>Shadows</u> <u>of the West</u> (circulated by the American Legion); Sax Rohmer's <u>Fu Manchu</u>; Peter B. Kyne's <u>The</u> <u>Pride of Palomar</u> and Wallace Irwin's <u>Seed of the Sun</u> (serialized in 1920 and issued as books a year later).

3. Negative stereotypes were slow to give way, often being helped to their demise by crisis, by American need, or by conclusive proof of falsity.

   a. When World War II came along, need for the Chinese allies was obvious. Official propaganda took a positive turn. Chinese Americans gained a better image.

   b. World War II increased the hate campaigns against Japanese Americans; but the activities of Nisei servicemen (especially the 442nd Regimental Combat Team) who volunteered out of prison-camp relocation centers and then served with heroism and loyalty, were a graphic

movies and T.V. programs and commercials).

Tom Englehardt, "Ambush at Kamikaze Pass" (contains an interesting analysis of more recent movie stereotypes)

demonstration which could not be
ignored.

E. From the very first, Asian Americans
made important contributions to the
building of America.

1. "Cracker's Battalions," Chinese   Moody, The Railroad Builders
laborers, proved to be excellent   Holbrook, The Story of American
workmen as they dispelled doubts of   Railroads
their ability to perform the heavy
manua- labor of building railroads.
(These men established a record for
the most miles of track laid in one
day by any track-laying crew.)

2. Japanese farmers reclaimed areas that   Hosokawa, Nisei: the Quiet
were considered unfit for cultiva-   Americans
tion, making them productive agri-
cultural lands. Japanese Americans
provided American tables with a rich
abundance of vegetables from their
truck farms and also helped to
beautify American communities with
ornamental gardens and landscaping
designs.

3. Asian Americans have a distinguished
record of American military service.

Study Outline	_Notes and Sources_
a. Seven Issei sailors on the battle-ship <u>Maine</u> died when the ship was sunk in Havana in 1898.	
b. Asian Americans served in World War I. Sing Kee, a Chinese American, won the D.S.C. for extraordinary bravery. (Even so, he remained ineligible for citizenship because he had not been born in America.)	Hosokawa, <u>Nisei: the Quiet Americans</u> (Page 327 has a picture of a decorated Navy veteran of World War I wearing his uniform in protest on the day of his evacuation in World War II.)
c. Japanese American servicemen captured the first prisoners of war, the crew of a Japanese midget submarine which had been put out of commission, as their largely Nisei unit (the 442nd) performed outstanding service in defense of Pearl Harbor.	(Many Nisei already in the Army were given transfers to the Enlisted Reserve "for the convenience of the government." Others were placed on permanent K.P. or stuck with other menial tasks within the States.)
d. Asian Americans, excepting Japanese Americans, performed alongside Whites in World War II service.	(After the battle of Midway, the 442nd was sent from Hawaii to the mainland.)
e. The Navy and Marines had a policy of not accepting Nisei, even before World War II.	
f. In World War II, Nisei found themselves reclassified as 4-F and 4-C	

(aliens not subject to military
service) under the Selective
Service System.

g. When Nisei were finally allowed to   Hosokawa, "Proof in Blood,"
volunteer for service, many more   Nisei: the Quiet Americans
volunteered than the Army would   (Segregation itself served to
at first accept. The volunteer   demonstrate the loyalty and
all-Nisei groups were opposed by   bravery of the Nisei on a scale
some who did not like the idea of   that would have been impossible
serving in segregated units.   had the Nisei troops been inte-

h. The 100th Battalion was the first   grated as many other Asian
Nisei unit to serve in the European   American servicemen were.)
theatre, landing at Oran, North
Africa, September 2, 1943.

i. The 442nd Regimental Combat Team   Inouye, Journey to Washington
(which included the 442nd Regiment,   (the autobiographical account
the 100th Battalion and other   of a hero who served with the
units) became the most famous Nisei   442nd)
unit, as it fought first in Italy,
then in France and then in Italy
again.

    (1) Among its military missions, the   (Such a record was extremely
bloodiest was the rescue of the   costly: in seven major cam-
1st Battalion of the 36th (Texas)   paigns, the 442nd suffered
Division 141st Infantry Regiment   9,486 casualties, more than
(the "Lost Battalion"), which had   300% of its original infantry

been cut off by the German

Army. (For this action, the

men of the 442nd were declared

"honorary Texans.")

(2) The 442nd captured Bruyeres,

which a 7th Army report

described as "the most vici-

ously fought-for town we had

encountered in our long march

against the Germans."

(3) In a plan to breach the defenses

of the Nazi Gothic Line in

northern Italy, the 442nd was

assigned a diversionary attack

on positions which had withheld

attack for five months and which

were deemed impregnable.

j. An equally important mission was

being performed in the Pacific

theatre by Nisei who, for security

reasons, were given no publicity.

(1) John Fujio Aiso was taken from

his Army assignment as a buck

private in truck repair, fur-

loughed to the enlisted reserve

strength, including 600 dead.
More than 18,000 individual
decorations for valor were won
by men of the 442nd, including
the Congressional Medal of Honor,
52 Distinguished Service Crosses,
and nearly 9,500 Purple Hearts.)

(Within five days these "decoys"
had achieved a complete victory.)

(Aiso had a brilliant record in-
cluding a law degree from Harvard
Law School and study in two
Japanese universities and legal

Study Outline	_Notes and Sources_

"for the convenience of the government" and reassigned as a hired civilian employee as head instructor of the new Fourth Army Intelligence School to teach Japanese language. Two other Nisei, Aki Oshida and Shig Kihara, were with Aiso as the first faculty for the school.

and business experience in Japanese-occupied Manchuria.)

(2) When the war began, a search was made for qualified speakers of Japanese among Nisei.

(3) Reports from the Pacific indicated that these Nisei linguists performed very well. General MacArthur's chief of intelligence, Maj. Gen. Charles A. Willoughby, remarked,

(Only 3% of Nisei interviewed were fluent in the language; 4% were considered fairly proficient; and an additional 3% knew enough Japanese to qualify as candidates for the school's intensive course.)

"Never before in history did an army know so much concerning its enemy, prior to actual engagement, as did the American Army during most of the Pacific campaigns."

Much of the credit for the truth of that statement is owed to the Nisei linguists.

(One achievement, for instance, was the translation of the entire Japanese battle plans for the naval battle of the Philippines, a copy of which had fallen into American hands by chance.)

(4) After the victory, the Nisei
linguists were assigned to
assist in occupation and re-
construction in Japan.

k. When Nisei proved such loyal and   (The feeling that it was unfair
capable soldiers, there was a re-   to be imprisoned one day and
versal of Selective Service policy,   forced into service the next is
which made Nisei subject to draft.   understandable.)
This policy met with a mixed
response.

l. In a White House ceremony honoring   (It was a hopeful note that with
the 442nd, President Truman said,   the beginning of hostilities
"You fought not only the enemy, but   with Communist China in the
you fought prejudice--and you won."   Korean War, there was no senseless

m. No other Asian Americans were able   reaction against Chinese Americans
to demonstrate their loyalty so   to match that of the anti-Nisei
conspicuously as a group again: action of World War II.)
the integrated service of the   (Individual bravery and dedicated
Korean War and of Vietnam included   service are still typical of Asian
able Americans of Oriental descent   Americans in uniform: Hershey
who performed as well as any of   Miyamura, who had fought with
their fellows, but there were no   outstanding bravery before his
more segregated groups such as the   capture in Korea, was awarded
"Go For Broke" 442nd.   the Congressional Medal of Honor
                                          upon his release when prisoners
                                          of war were exchanged.)

F. Many Asian Americans have made outstanding contributions to their

    country and to the world in all fields of human achievement.

    1. Japanese Americans in science:

    - Dr. Thomas T. Omozi, aerospace scientist

    - Dr. Kiyo Tomiyasu, authority on radio microwaves

    - David H. Furukawa, research engineer specializing in water

      desalinization

    - Dr. Jin H. Kinoshita, opthalmologist who has made important research

      discoveries

    - Dr. Newton Wesley, who helped perfect and popularize plastic contact

      lenses

    - Dr. Paul Terasaki, U.C.L.A., professor of surgery, who played a key

      role in heart transplants

    - Dr. Chihiro Kikuchi, mathematician, physicist, and atomic engineer,

      who has made important discoveries in maser action and space

      communication

    - Dr. Kazumi Kasuga, specialist in tuberculosis and Indian health with

      the U.S. Public Health Service

    - Dr. Hideo Noguchi, Issei, conqueror of yellow fever and discoverer of

      the organism which causes syphilis

    - Dr. Jokichi Takamine, Issei, discoverer of adrenaline.

    2. Chinese Americans in science:

    - Dr. Chien Chiung Wu, considered the world's foremost woman physicist

    - Dr. Chen Ning Yang and Dr. Tsung Dao Lee, winners of the Nobel Physics

      Prize in 1957

- Dr. Ju Chin Chu, aerospace expert and consultant on important space projects

- Dr. Choh Hao Li, noted biochemist and one of four brothers listed in American Men of Science

- Dr. M. C. Chang, biologist who helped perfect "the pill"

- Dr. M. C. Li, noted cancer researcher.

3. In politics Oriental Americans are beginning to provide leadership as their outstanding abilities are recognized:

- Wing F. Ong, the first Chinese American to sit in a state legislature (in Arizona, 1946)

- William D. Soo Hoo, elected mayor of Oxnard, California, in 1966

- Hiram Fong of Hawaii, the first Chinese American senator

- John F. Aiso, the first Nisei jurist in California

- Mrs. Patsy Mink, Hawaii's first Japanese American woman to become an attorney, who also became a Congresswoman from that state

- Dan Inouye, war hero in World War II, who became a senator from Hawaii

- Spark M. Matsunaga, another veteran, who was elected Congressman from Hawaii.

4. Scholars:

- Achilles Fong, of Harvard

- Samuel Ichiye Hayakawa, semanticist and Negro rights champion, president of San Francisco State College (some of his writings on language are standard texts in semantics and linguistics courses)

- Paul K. T. Sih, Asian studies

- Chih Meng, Asian studies

- Francis L. K. Hsu, anthropology

- Kuangchi C. Chang, classic Chinese art and literature.

5. Architecture, Arts and Entertainment:

   - Henry T. Ushijima, Chicago movie producer, member of the board of
     governors, Academy of Television Arts and Sciences

   - Minoru Yamasaki, Japanese American, one of America's most outstanding
     architects

   - Ieoh Ming Pei, Chinese American, noted for his architectural designs

   - Doug Kingman, Chinese American water colorist

   - Paul Horiuchi, noted painter

   - Yosuke W. (Nick) Nakamo, architect and engineer

   - Yasua Matsui, architect

   - Mine Okubu, artist

   - George Tsutakawa, sculptor

   - Isamu Noguchi, sculptor

   - Tomi Kanazawa, opera and concert singer

   - Uasuo Kuniyoshi, artist

   - Harry Ayao Osaki, silversmith

   - Sono Osato, ballerina

   - Seiji Ozawa, conductor of the San Francisco Symphony

   - Yuriko Amemiya, dancer

   - Don Ho, singer and entertainer

   - Chiang Yee, painter and writer

   - Chou Wen Chung, musical composer

   - Yi-Kwei Sze, concert soloist

- Kuangchi C. Chang, poet, architect and expert in classical Chinese art and literature.

Cinema: Sessue Hayakawa, James Shigeta, Pat Suzuki, Nancy Kwan, Yukio Aoyama, Benji Okubo, Arthur Kaischatsu, James Wong Howe, Miyoshi Umeki, Harold Sakata, Mako.

6. Entrepreneurs, Businessmen, Agriculturists:

- Kyutaro Abiko, banker and publisher of the newspaper Nichi Bei, land company organizer

- Jinnosuke Kobata, founder of the Japanese nursery business in Los Angeles area

- Kotaro Suto, one of the developers of Miami Beach

- Kosaku Sowarda, flower breeder, developer of thousands of new varieties

- George Shima, pioneer of land reclamation in the Sacramento delta area

- Hachiro Onuki (Hutchlon Ohnick), Arizona pioneer in supplying gas and electric power

- Masajiro Furuya, Northwestern banker, merchant and manufacturer

- Harry Sotaro Kawabe, Alaskan businessman

- Masuo Yasui, Oregon entrepreneur

- Saito Saibara (who was a member of parliament in Japan before coming to America), doubled American rice yields with a strain which he introduced to American agriculture (the Saibara-Asahi strain, as it is now known)

- Masahara Kondo, Issei, pioneer of the Southern California fishing industry

- Kenji Fujii, flowergrower of Hayward, California

- Gerald Tsai, Jr., financier.

7. Athletes:

    - Ford Hiroshi Konno, swimmer

    - Tommy Kono, weightlifter, repeat Olympic champion

    - Yoshihiro Uchida, Judo-educator, Olympic coach

    - Chi Cheng, fastest female runner in the world (has competed for Nationalist China)

    - C. K. Yang, U.C.L.A. athlete who competed in Olympic games for Nationalist China

    - Dr. Sammy Lee, Korean American Olympic diving champion.

8. Civic Service and Civil Rights:

    - William M. Murutani, a Philadelphia lawyer, who was invited to speak when the Supreme Court heard the Loving case and rendered the important decision on miscegenation

    - Dr. Thomas T. Yatabe, a founder of the Japanese American Citizens League

    - Saburo Kido, attorney and Nisei leader, president of the wartime JACL

    - George Kiyoshi Togasaki, 1968-69 president of Rotary International

    - Henry Kasai, successful lobbyist whose persuasion achieved legislative breakthroughs in Utah

    - Mike Masaoka, lobbyist and civil rights leader.

9. Writers (literary artists are increasing in numbers; the four listed here represent four different ethnic and cultural origins; other representative writers are also listed in the reference column of the units):

    (See also Iwasaki, "Response and Change for the Asian in America: A Survey of Asian American Literature" in Tachiki, Wong, Odo and Wong's Roots: An Asian American Reader.)

- Jose Garcia Villa, Filipino American mystic, painter and poet

- Lin Yutang, Chinese American whose writings include essays, novels and other forms

- Shisei Tsuneishi, Japanese American poet

- Kim Yong Ik, young Korean American novelist.

G. Recent U.S. involvement in Asia has brought an increasing awareness of a number of Asian countries from which immigrants have come or are coming as refugees, students, war brides, and as suppliers of needed scientific and technological skills.

Kim, The Martyred (Kim came from Korea as a college student. There are excerpts from his novel, set in the Korean War, in Haslam's Forgotten Pages of American Literature.)

1. U.S. involvement in Asia has brought students from a number of countries to learn military technology in a variety of American military schools.

Pearl Buck, "Home Girl," and "Mr. Right," Hearts Come Home and Other Stories

Nakamura and Yoshimura, "The Nature of G.I. Racism," "G.I.'s and Asian Women" in Tachika, Wong, Odo and Wong's Roots: An Asian American Reader (deals with negative stereotypes and racism among U.S. servicemen)

2. U.S. servicemen have gained a first-hand acquaintance with Asian peoples from Korea, Vietnam, Thailand and a number of other countries, besides Taiwan and Japan. Though such acquaintances were often made under unfavorable circumstances accompanying war and military service itself, many Americans returned with an increased respect for Oriental

Chang, "Garden of My Childhood," in Faderman and Bradshaw's Speaking for Ourselves (a poem dealing with the refugee experience)

36

cultures and for the people whom they
had come to know as fellow human
beings.

3. G.I.'s came to a better understanding
   of Japanese appreciation of beauty
   (and perhaps of Japanese art and
   poetry) when they saw the perfect
   symmetry of Mt. Fuji; observed the
   beauty of the full moon on a summer
   night in Southern Japan; listened to
   the sounds of happy voices coming
   from a small boat in the otherwise
   quiet darkness of night along the
   seacoast; or when they visited Osaka

   shrines, Nara's great Buddha, the

   Bronze Buddha at Kamakura or the   Kipling wrote,

   Golden Pavilion in Kyoto.   And whoso will, from
                                                      Pride released,
4. In post-war Japan and Korea, once the   Condemning neither
                                                      creed nor priest,
   indignity and inhumanity of war was   May feel the soul of
                                                      all the East
   not the first consideration, many   About him at Kamakura.

   young Americans cured themselves of

   prejudices: the beauty of Oriental

   women, the strength and intelligence

   of handsome young men, and the dig-

   nity and wisdom of the elderly were

impossible to reconcile with the

negative stereotypes and propaganda

Americans had grown to accept.

5. Each country had its own beauty:

    the mountains and valleys of Korea,

    cherry blossoms in spring, rivers

    swollen in monsoon season or clear at

    other times; the Buddhist ruins of

    Thailand, boats on canals; the

    varying costumes--the Korean elder's

    hat, the Japanese kimono and geta,

    the cheongsam on a pretty Vietnamese

    girl.

III Conclusion

The post-World War II era was a more pleasant time for Asian Americans
in many ways (despite the red tape and injustice which many Japanese Americans met in trying to regain property which they had lost in relocation).
Chinese Americans no longer faced the discriminatory pre-1943 immigration
laws; and Japanese Americans were successful lobbyists (partly due to
American sense of shame at the obvious discrimination and injustice of World
War II relocation) in getting much better immigration laws passed.

The immediate effect was the immigration of a large number of Oriental
women. The old "picture bride" system and the separation of husband and wife
(husband in America, wife in Asia) were no longer necessary. Most of the
Chinese immigrants were young women, with or without children. Many of them
came from Hong Kong where they had fled at the takeover of mainland China
by a Communist government. Chinese dependents were often considered well-to-
do in the Orient. But there were problems in this era. Husbands and wives
were often shocked to find each other grown old when in memory each had remained young to the other, as on the day of parting. Sons who had grown up
in a modern China were estranged from their fathers who remembered only the
old. Wives who had lived well in the Orient on the money provided by their
American husbands were often unpleasantly amazed at the daily routine of hard
work those husbands faced (and which the wives were now to share).

GLOSSARY

The following glossary may be helpful in studying Asian Americans.

Aliens Ineligible for Citizenship: Immigrants, many from Asia, who were ineligible for naturalization and citizenship usually because of their race

Alien Land Laws: Laws passed by several state legislatures, especially in the West, to prevent the ownership of property by immigrants from Asia

American Loyalty League: A short-lived pioneer Japanese American organization formed in 1918 to promote integration and participation in American life

Asian Exclusion Laws: A series of laws beginning with the Chinese Exclusion Act of 1882 and culminating in the 1924 Asian Exclusion Act, designed to limit or prevent immigration from Asia

Asiatic Exclusion League: A labor-dominated organization formed in California to deny entrance to immigrants of Asian origin

Banana: The metaphorical equivalent of an "Uncle Tom" or "Oreo"--"Yellow on the outside, white on the inside"

Buddhism: An Asian religion based on the teachings of Gautama Buddha

Cable Act: An act passed in 1923 which provided that female citizens would lose their citizenship if they married aliens not eligible for citizenship; widowed or divorced white women could regain their citizenship, whereas widowed or divorced Asian Americans could not

Celestials: In times past, a term of derision for Chinese Americans

Chinaman: A name applied to immigrants from China and their descendants in America; no longer in popular usage

Chinaman's Chance: An American expression which means that there is no chance at all

Chinatown: A community of people of Chinese descent within a larger non-Chinese community, the largest in the U.S. being those of San Francisco, New York and Los Angeles

Chinese American Citizens Alliance: A basically integrationist organization formed by young American-born citizens

Chinese Consolidated Benevolent Association: Successor to the Six Companies; an organization which maintained a somewhat nationalistic leadership in the Chinese American community until recent years

Confucianism: The philosophical system of Confucious and his followers; the basis of much of the Chinese ethical and cultural system

Coolie Brokers: Men who recruited penniless laborers or "coolies" in China for American employers

Cracker's Battalions: Chinese immigrant railroad construction crews

Enryo: A Japanese concept; modesty in the presence of one's superiors

Evacuation Claims Act: An act passed in 1948 which provided for repayment of some of the losses of Japanese Americans incurred in relocation; the average rate of settlement was about 10 cents per dollar value lost

Executive Order 9066: The order of February 19, 1942, providing for evacuation of Japanese Americans (anyone of 1/8 or more Japanese blood) from many areas of the West to relocation camps

Ga-man: A Japanese concept; sticking things out, as in marriage; bearing up under pain or adversity; suppression of emotion

Geisha: A Japanese professional singing and dancing girl

Genro: In Japanese, an elder statesman

Gentlemen's Agreement: An agreement between the U.S. and Japan in which Japan agreed to limit emigration in return for equal treatment of school children and other Japanese in America

Giri: A Japanese word relating to role position, with a connotation of moral obligation or duty to family and community

Gook: A term of derogation applied, often by servicemen, to Asians

Haiku: A very short verse form originated by Japanese poets

Ha-ku-jin: A Japanese expression meaning white man

Ha zu ka shi: A norm of social control: "others will laugh at you"

Hi-ge: Japanese tradition which holds that self praise or praise of family in public is in bad taste

Internment: The imprisonment of Japanese Americans, citizens or not, during World War II

Issei: A first generation immigrant born in Japan

Jap: Along with Nip, an expression of derogation in common usage in World War II

Japanese American Citizen's League (JACL): A Nisei-Sansei organization which represents the Japanese American minority and which is basically assimilationist in its stance

Japanese Association: An organization which provided protection and services to Issei in American communities

Kabuki: A type of Japanese theatrical entertainment

Kenjinkai: Prefectural organizations for Japanese Americans who shared the same dialect, sect, and customs

Kibei: Nisei who were sent to Japan for a part of their training and education, especially in the 1920-1940 era, when it was a popular practice to send at least one son to Japan

Ki-chi-gai: In Japanese, aberrant or crazy behavior

Kimono: A loose robe worn as an outer garment by Japanese men and women

The Lost Colony: The Wakamatsu colony of pioneer Japanese immigrants who came to California in 1869

McCarran-Walter Immigration Bill: A bill passed in 1952 which made provision for naturalization and citizenship for Issei and for a token Japanese immigration quota, repealing the Asian Exclusion Act of 1924

Middle Kingdom: China, traditionally regarded by Chinese as the best culture, with all others considered more or less barbaric

Native Sons of the Golden State: An early Chinese American organization with integrationist aims; a forerunner to the Chinese American Citizens Alliance

Naturalization Act: An act passed in 1790 which limited the right of citizenship to free whites

Nihonmachi: A Japanese area within a city, similar to Chinatown to the Chinese Americans

Nikkei: A term referring to Japanese Americans, more inclusive than the terms Issei, Nisei, and Sansei

Nippon: Japan

Nipponese: Japanese

Nisei: Those born in America to Issei parents; second generation Japanese Americans

Oyabun and Ko-bun: Japanese parent and child; a relationship between employer and employee

Oya-Koko: A Japanese expression meaning filial piety

Papa-san: Japanese head of a household

Picture Brides: Brides selected by Asian Americans through correspondence or by arrangements made with go betweens and married in a type of proxy ceremony

Pig Trade: The commerce in Chinese laborers bound for America, in which the workers often faced conditions similar to those found by the black slaves in the middle passage of the slave trade

Queue: The "pigtail" which Chinese Americans wore prior to 1911 as a symbol of bondage to the Chinese Manchu dynasty

Red Guards: A group of San Francisco Chinatown youths who have made protests against the poverty and neglect in their community, and who described themselves as being styled after the Black Panthers

Relocation Camps: Prison camps in the United States interior where Japanese Americans were interned in World War II

Sansei: Third generation Japanese Americans born to Nisei parents

Shi-ka-ta-ga-nai: A Japanese expression meaning "it can't be helped"; the idea that one's fate is tied to forces beyond his control

Shintoism: A Japanese religion or cult respected by adherents of several faiths which includes a reverence to the spirits of imperial ancestors and historical personages

Six Companies: A quasi-governmental organization formed to provide services for the Chinese American community and which, in turn, exacted loyalty, and submission to its leadership

Sokka-Gakkai: A nationalistic religious movement which originated in Japan

Soldier Brides Bill: A bill which was amended to allow Japanese spouses and children to enter the U.S.

Tanomoshi: A Japanese expression meaning to rely on or to depend on

Taoism: A philosophy which enabled early Chinese Immigrants to react passively to mistreatment in America

Tongs: Organizations in the Chinese American community which served as banking institutions and which provided fellowship and services; tongs kept alive old rivalries and for a time engaged in protection rackets, but later reverted to the role of social lodges

War Brides: Brides brought by American soldiers from abroad, a number being
    Asian

Yellow Peril: A slogan reflecting fear that Asian Americans would "breed
    like rabbits" and become a majority of the population

PART TWO: ASIAN AMERICAN CONFLICT

I   Introduction

Many of the "differences" which Whites saw in Oriental Americans--taste
in foods, choice of entertainment, clothing styles, and so on--were really
very much like the usual differences various ethnic groups brought from
Europe. To new immigrants such "differences" were "samenesses," giving them
a sense of security and of identity.

But Americans, like others, were largely intolerant of such differences.
Though such differences were not unusual, they were still points of conflict.

The Oriental immigrant--and to some extent the second generation American of Oriental descent--had the usual cultural and linguistic conflicts to
deal with. And, like many other newcomers, he usually found open to him the
jobs that earlier arrivals did not really want.

More to the point, the Asian American was visible. No matter how he
dressed, he was usually identifiable as non-Anglo-Saxon. And visible
minorities are the most obvious candidates for discrimination. The Asian-
American became a prime target of organized labor and of politicians willing
to prostitute themselves and the election process, as they bought votes and
sold out justice with their "yellow peril" slogans of fear and hate.

Asian-American reaction varied. Where it was possible to do so, or
where it served his own interest, the Asian American removed himself from
the scene of greatest conflict. Where the law denied him protection, he
banded with others like himself for strength; later, he lobbied for the
passage of equitable laws.

The immigrant who retained his Japanese or Chinese citizenship received
some support from the country of his birth.

One way the Asian American found to beat the system was to become more
efficient than Whites in using the system itself: in becoming more efficient
farmers, or better businessmen, or in taking more complete advantage of educational opportunities.

II   Guide and Sourcebook

Study Outline	*Notes and Sources*
A. It was a type of conflict--the struggle	Buck, The Good Earth (presents
to make a living--which brought the	a picture of some of the natural
Oriental immigrant to America, where	calamities, such as drought,

44

Study Outline	_Notes and Sources_

he thought to find means to better conditions for his family.

which might make it imperative for villagers to look elsewhere to support families and homes)

1. Ties to home and family might over-populate some areas of China, creating areas of poverty. Floods and droughts might alternate, leaving great need in their wakes.

2. Japan was faced with the problem of a limited area for support of her population.

3. In making the decision to leave his ancestral home, there was an inner conflict which each man had as he weighed the relative benefits of staying with his family or going to America with its better possibility of wealth.

Mitchison, The Overseas Chinese

B. The journey itself was usually un-pleasant, often dangerous, for the mi-grating Asian.

1. Conditions on boats used in the "pig trade" were often comparable to those on slave ships of the middle passage.

Mitchison, The Overseas Chinese

2. Many (sometimes half) of the pas-sengers died.

Hosokawa, Nisei: The Quiet Americans

Study Outline	Notes and Sources

3. Coolie brokers recruited penniless laborers to sell into virtual slavery.

4. In China, some who did not wish to emigrate were kidnapped by brokers and sold in San Francisco or Hawaii.

(Sometimes American employers paid their passage in return for bond-service, which was actually very close to slavery.)

C. Once in America, the Chinese were almost immediately subject to private and institutional discrimination and injustice. Chinese were the first Asian Americans to become scapegoats in economic competition.

1. The gold rush brought the first large group of Chinese to America. By 1851, 25,000 had arrived.

2. A long series of discriminatory laws began with California's imposition of a $20.00 per month tax on all foreign miners. The effect was to depopulate Chinese miners' camps.

(As a result many Chinese moved into San Francisco to go into business for themselves, carpentering, washing and ironing, operating restaurants and hotels.)

3. With failure of the first law to achieve the desired effect (to keep Chinese working in the mines but to tax them heavily for the privilege), a new tax on foreign miners was levied in 1852, this time at $4.00 per month.

(Chinese reaction was much more favorable; they paid 85% of the total tax collected under this law, though Irish outnumbered Chinese miners and Germans were nearly as numerous.)

D. Prejudice flared into violence in the gold camps.

1. There was a fear that Chinese would take "white man's" gold.

2. Whites derided Chinese, nicknaming them "Celestials," ridiculing their Oriental dress and their queues (pigtails).

3. Problems with bullies and vigilantes arose: Chinese were easy prey for the bullies because they could not or would not fight back.

4. Because of pressures from miners, the Chinese began to move into businesses, where a demand for their ability slowed persecution. Cooking and laundering began to emerge as main means of support.

5. Even businessmen were not immune to violence and injustice: a notorious madame in one of the West's livelier boomtowns gained ownership of the town's best new building for her own business by the simple expedient of driving out the Chinese owner.

Bret Harte, "The Latest Chinese Outrage" and "Wan Lee, The Pagan," in Anderson and Wright's The Dark and Tangled Path: Race in America (Joaquin Murieta rode into Chinese camps, tied victims by their queues, and tortued them for the gold they had.) Twain, Roughing It (Mention is made of a practice of requiring a $10 immunization of all Chinese upon arrival in San Francisco as a discouragement to immigration.)

Study Outline	_Notes and Sources_

6. Chinese were not permitted to testify in court on the grounds that no oath could be administered to a "heathen."

Lyman, The Asian in the West (A California judge ruled that Chinese were "Indians"; and Indians could not give testimony in California courts for a number of years.)

E. With the demand for railroad construction workers, Chinese came to America in greater numbers.

1. By 1870 there were 63,000 Chinese in the U.S., with 99% of them on the West Coast.

Moody, The Railroad Builders

2. A new challenge arose: many Americans (employers and workers alike) did not believe that Chinese workers, who were small by American standards, would be able to perform the heavy tasks required in building railroads. Chinese labor was also to build the Northwest Pacific Railroad and was to be the chief labor force on the Southern Pacific.

Holbrook, The Story of American Railroads

Sung, Mountain of Gold (In answer, it was a Chinese crew which established the record for the most miles of track laid in a single day in a competition with the rival Union Pacific crew of Irishmen.)

3. With the end of construction on the transcontinental railroad, in 1869, there was widespread unemployment-- with a large concentration of laborers in the West where the railroad construction crews had met. American labor blamed its troubles on

the Chinese, who were regarded as unfair competition, especially when the
depression of 1873 came.

F. Labor violence was directed against
    Chinese workers; anti-Chinese legis-
    lation followed.

    1. In 1870 a law was passed in Cali-   Sandmeyer, The Anti-Chinese
        fornia requiring 500 cubic feet of   Movement in California
        air space per lodger, in an attempt
        to harass Chinese who were living in
        confined areas.

    2. In 1871 stores were looted and 21
        Chinese were killed by a lynch mob in
        Los Angeles.

    3. Dennis Kearney waged a campaign
        against Chinese, accusing them of
        accepting slave wages and of re-
        placing white workers. His speeches
        ended with the slogan, "The Chinese
        must go!"

    4. Chinese were attacked by mobs.   Lyman, The Asian in the West

    5. In June of 1876 a violent attack was
        made on the Chinese at Truckee.

    6. In 1877 employers of Chinese labor in
        Chico, California, received threaten-
        ing letters. In March 1877, six

tenant farmers were attacked (five were killed). The man who confessed to the murders claimed to be under orders from the Workingman's Party. In July 1877, 25 washhouses were burned and occupants were shot in Chico. Riots followed. No Chinese were safe on the streets.

7. In 1877 Chinese were restricted by law from becoming naturalized citizens.

8. In 1878 the entire Chinese population of Truckee was rounded up and driven out of town.

9. Professional agitators created a public image of the Chinese as a deceitful, sly, and menacing group who worshipped idols.

10. In 1882, the Chinese Exclusion Act was passed. The effect of the 1882 law, which was passed after the Burlingame treaty had been revised, was to suspend immigration of Chinese labor for ten years.

(Congress had passed a Chinese Exclusion Act in 1879, but President Hayes had vetoed it because it violated the Burlingame treaty with China. Then in 1881 Congress passed a bill suspending Chinese immigration for 20 years;

11. In 1885 at Rock Springs, Wyoming, 28 Chinese were massacred, many others were wounded and hundreds were driven from their homes.

12. In 1886 another brutal massacre took place at Log Cabin, Oregon.

13. Denver, Colorado, was the scene of mob action which destroyed every Chinese laundry, business and home.

14. The Scott Act of 1888 redefined Chinese to further limit Oriental entry. This act also had the effect of denying re-entry to Chinese Americans who had gone to China for a visit, thus locking out about 20,000 men who had intended to return to jobs and businesses in America.

15. The 1888 Geary Act was even harsher than previous legislation, practically stripping Chinese of any protection in courts, requiring all Chinese to obtain a certificate of eligibility to remain in the U.S.

16. The 1882 Chinese Exclusion Act was extended regularly every ten years. In 1902 its extension guaranteed it

President Arthur vetoed it as unreasonable and excessive.)

McGraw, The Anti-Chinese Riots of 1885

History of the Union Pacific Coal Mines 1868 to 1940 (Chapter VI "Chinese Riot and Massacre of September 2, 1885.")

The phrase "Not a Chinaman's chance!" was born of this period. When this law was tested in the Supreme Court, it was upheld, though Chief Justice Field acknowledged that it violated the treaties of 1868 and 1880 as well as being contrary to the Constitution. Field justified it on

to live ten years beyond the twenty
that President Arthur had vetoed as
being excessive. The 1902 extension
was strengthened by acts of 1904,
1911, 1912 and 1913.

17. In 1901, 800 unionists and 200
politicians attended the Chinese
Exclusion Convention in San Francisco.

18. In 1917 all Asians except Japanese
were barred from immigrating.

19. A 1921 act stated that alien-born
women who married American citizens
did not thereby automatically become citizens.

20. A law of 1924 excluded all further
immigration of aliens ineligible for
citizenship, with the intent of preventing any further immigration of
Orientals. This law also worked a
hardship on students. Under this
law only graduate students (those
who were working on master or doc-
torate degrees) were admitted to
study in America.

grounds of public interest and
necessity.

Shen Tso-Chien, What Chinese
Exclusion Really Means

(A few Japanese passed out leaf-
lets asking that the Japanese be
left alone, but not defending
the Chinese.)

Alien-born wives could not enter
the United States; some families
were separated by this law for
many years.

Devine, American Immigration
Policy 1924-1952
Other laws had made it extremely
difficult for the Chinese American man to have a wife; the law
of 1924 virtually condemned him
to celibacy.

21. In the midst of all this legislating against Chinese Americans, segregated schools were established for Chinese American children.

22. Under the immigration laws subsequent to 1882, only a few categories of Chinese were eligible to enter the U.S. For many years a tourist from China might expect a routine wait of weeks in what had all the earmarks of a poorly-kept jail before being allowed to proceed with his travels in America. Students were also subject to the same treatment, as immigration officials pursued a policy of deliberate harassment, keeping to the spirit as well as to the letter of American law which related to Chinese.

(These categories included businessmen, professionals and students.)

G. There was a basis in fact for the fears which labor and businessmen felt; though such fears and such fact could hardly justify the excessive laws which were generated against these Asian-Americans.

Study Outline	*Notes and Sources*

1. Willingness of the Chinese to work long hours with efficiency even without supervision created a demand for them as workers, often in preference to Whites. Whites did lose jobs to Chinese immigrants.

2. Chinese were used as strikebreakers by unscrupulous employers (often unwittingly).

3. Many Chinese were possessed of a keen business sense; Chinese have traditionally operated much of the business of Asia, even outside their own country.

    Mitchison, The Overseas Chinese
(In a debate in the Senate in 1902 on the usefulness of Chinese in the Philippines, Governor Taft said,

The Chinese comes into this country and labors, say for twelve silver dollars a month. Out of that, the local saying is, he saves $16 to $18. At any rate, he is not there for more than three or four months before he has capital to set up a store, and when he sets up a store, the Filipino who has the store next to him is driven out of business.)

4. The frugality of Chinese Americans became a sore point with Whites who envied their ability to "get ahead."

H. Chinese reaction was tempered by several factors.

1. Protests by the Chinese government were not as effective as they might have been because (a) China herself was experiencing internal difficulties at home, (b) European powers were threatening China's sovereignty as they extended their own

(U.S. foreign policy was generally favorable to China; the treatment of Chinese Americans was the sorest point of U.S.-Chinese relations.)

Study Outline	*Notes and Sources*

imperialistic designs in the Orient,
(c) China was interested in main-
taining the good will of the U.S.

2. Reaction of Chinese Americans was
   tempered by various Oriental philosophies which taught acceptance,
   but it was determined more largely
   by the fact that Chinese-Americans
   were vastly outnumbered by white
   Americans who opposed them.

(See Section A of the "Identity"
unit for some philosophical
teachings.)

3. The first Chinese reaction to America
   was to work hard to please employers;
   when such tactics (evidence of respect for authority) did not contribute to amicable relations with
   white laborers, the Chinese immigrant
   was forced to use other methods to
   achieve his aims.

4. Voluntary segregation was the Chinese
   defense, a self-defense against the
   possibility of greater hostility
   which might occur if competition
   were to continue.

5. If the white man begrudged him a job,
   he set up his own business and became

Sung, "Honorable Deception,"
Mountain of Gold

his own employer. If American courts
denied him justice, he bypassed them
and set up his own organization for
settling differences.

6. The Six Companies, established in the
    1850's, became a dominant factor in
    Chinese American life, controlling
    travel to and from China, financing
    businesses, meting out punishment,
    and representing Chinese in court
    (or serving as a separate Chinese
    American judicial system).

7. Chinese American urbanization grew
    as a means of protection from perse-
    cution. The Chinatowns of San
    Francisco, New York City, Los Angeles
    and other cities developed. (Chinese
    Americans had been involved as agri-
    cultural laborers for a time, sup-
    plying a tenth of the farm workers
    in California by 1870, a third by
    1880 and half by 1884.)

8. The growth of Chinatowns was only
    partially voluntary; white restric-
    tions on residential areas were a

(Chinese also exercised their
own form of civil disobedience
to gain citizenship and to bring
in "sons" from China, in evasion
of immigration laws.)

Lang, Chinese Family and Society

(In 1880, 22% of Chinese Americans
were living in urban areas, with
the other 78% in rural areas;
by 1960, 99% of Chinese Americans were living in urban areas.)

factor in creating these segregated
communities.

9. Voluntary segregation continues in
    Chinatowns today, after much of the
    white antagonism which made segrega-
    tion necessary has ceased to exist.
    Chinatowns are actually growing,
    partially due to increased Chinese
    immigration. New immigrants tend
    to settle among friends or relatives.

Yuan, "Voluntary Segregation:
A Study of New York's China-
town," in Kurokawa's Minority
Responses

10. The Chinese American Citizens
    Alliance, organized in 1900, has
    fought for Chinese rights, against
    attempts to disfranchise Chinese
    Americans, against business dis-
    crimination.

I. Practices within the Chinese American
    community led to personal or group
    conflicts.

1. The effect of immigration laws pro-
    duced unhappy social conditions
    within Chinese American society. As
    women were largely excluded, many
    bachelors led lives of involuntary
    celibacy; many of the women who did

(See the "Identity" section for
other details and references.)
(In Chicago in 1934 there were
5,000 males and 40 female Chinese
Americans according to one report.)

come to the U.S. were forced into
prostitution or polyandry.

2. These same laws separated families;
    the foreign-born sons of Chinese
    American fathers as well as the
    country to which they had come.

Lee Yu-Hwa, "The Monument," in
Haslam's Forgotten Pages of
American Literature (shows
change in China)

3. Chinese brought in as indentured im-
    migrants soon became slaves to their
    own countrymen who ruled them with an
    influence that was not understood by
    outside observers.

4. The Tongs, secret societies, which
    were originally fraternal organiza-
    tions, grew to take the place of
    family life for bachelors. The Tongs
    operated a number of enterprises
    which were outside the law: prosti-
    tution, gambling and drugs. Later,
    they were associated with "protec-
    tion" rackets.

Glick, Swords of Silence:
Chinese Secret Societies, Past
and Present
Dillon, The Hatchet Men (Tong
wars brought discredit to
Chinese Americans; Chinese
Americans began to acquire
criminal reputations when local
police were called in to break
up the wars. There have been no
Tong wars for many years now.)

5. The old elite, composed of executives
    of the clans, hui kuans and secret
    societies, continue to exercise a
    benevolent but despotic authority
    at the expense of their subjects.

J. With the precedent of early anti-
Chinese violence and legal aggression,
prejudice and discrimination against
Japanese Americans was inevitable.

1. It was not long before the old anti-   Lyman, The Asian in the West
Chinese slogans were being associated
with the Japanese-American, along
with a few new twists.

The old ones:

Orientals, as a race, could not be   The new twists:
assimilated into white American   Japan itself was a warlike,
society. Japanese (Chinese) life-   imperialistic, land-hungry
style was mysterious and, therefore, country; hence, Japanese immi-
suspicious. Japanese (Chinese) had   gration might be only a front
sly, greedy, dishonest personal   for Japanese imperialistic
habits. Japanese (Chinese) competi- expansion.
tion would disrupt the American   The Japanese lacked humility
economy. Japanese (Chinese) "breed (which should obviously accom-
like rabbits"; their fecundity would pany any skin color besides
fill America's living space with   white).
"foreigners."

2. In 1893 the San Francisco school   Takahashi, "Nisei, Nisei!" in
board adopted a resolution to send   Faderman and Bradshaw's Speaking
Japanese American children to the   for Ourselves (Theme of racial
Chinese school. Japanese Consul   inferiority and prejudiced
Chinda protested this action.   stereotype is relevant.)

Study Outline	*Notes and Sources*

Following Chinda's protest, the board rescinded the resolution.

(The California political code allowed for the establishment of "separate schools for children of Mongolian or Chinese descent.")

3. In 1900 San Francisco Mayor James D. Phelan quarantined Chinese and Japanese sections of the city and ordered mass inoculations of Orientals, following a report of the discovery of a Chinese victim of bubonic plague. Japanese community leaders protested that this action was designed to put them out of business.

4. In 1901 The Japanese Association of America was organized. With its close ties to the Japanese government, this organization could bring some effective political and diplomatic pressure to its support.

(Japan did not have China's internal problems and external threats; Japan was a rising power instead.)

5. The 1900-1908 period brought the greatest Japanese immigration, increasing Japanese American visibility and heightening anti-Japanese feeling and expression.

(139,103 entered in this period.)

6. Politicians exploited fear of the "yellow peril."

Hosokawa, Nisei: The Quiet Americans (has pictures of

7. The San Francisco Chronicle's
    February 23, 1905 headline read:
    "THE JAPANESE INVASION, THE PROBLEM
    OF THE HOUR." This was followed by
    stories published under lurid head-
    lines such as, "JAPANESE A MENACE TO
    AMERICAN WOMEN," and "CRIME AND
    POVERTY GO HAND IN HAND WITH ASIATIC
    LABOR."

8. The California legislature unani-
    mously passed a resolution asking
    Congress to "limit and diminish the
    further immigration of Japanese."

9. The labor-dominated Asiatic Exclusion
    League was formed in San Francisco
    and had a membership of more than
    75,000 within a year.

10. Mayor Eugene Schmitz of San Francisco
    ordered school segregation.

11. In 1905 the San Francisco school
    board decided to send Japanese pupils
    to an enlarged Oriental school so
    that white children would not be
    "affected by association with pupils
    of the Mongolian race."

political posters and accounts
of campaigns)
Hayakawa's short verse, "A
Matter of Linguistics," in
Haslam's Forgotten Pages of
American Literature

(The resolution described the
Japanese immigrants as transients
who did not buy land or build
houses and who did not contribute
to the growth of the state.
Later legislatures tried to keep
them from buying and building.)

12. In 1906 San Francisco principals were directed to send "all Chinese, Japanese and Korean children" to the Oriental School. (Japan had just humbled Russia in war. Japanese governmental pressure was brought to bear again. President Theodore Roosevelt sent Secretary of Commerce and Labor Victor H. Metcalf to work out a better solution. A compromise was effected: overage Japanese students--such as teenagers who because of the language problem were studying primary grades--were sent to separate schools; Japanese American students who were studying at their own age level were enrolled in the regular public schools.)

Lyman, *The Asian in the West*

13. In 1906 Alien Land Acts had been passed in Washington, Oregon and California.

14. In 1908 the "Gentlemen's Agreement" was negotiated to reduce Japanese immigration. This agreement was in effect until 1924.

(These acts aimed at divesting Chinese and Japanese of their land holdings and at preventing them from purchasing other parcels.)

(In 1909, after the new limitations took effect, only 3,275 came in. In the rush to get in before the

15. Upon being barred from labor unions and the possibility of working in the city, Japanese turned to agriculture. Japanese American success in farming created new jealousies and fears.

"Gentlemen's Agreement took effect, 16,418 Japanese immigrants came to the U.S.)

16. The 1913 California Alien Land Law was passed "to prevent aliens who are ineligible to citizenship from owning land in California."

17. Kyutaro Abiko and others found a legal loophole in the Alien Land Law: alien Japanese could buy farmland in the name of their American-born children. Soon children in diapers were legal owners of property which was managed and operated for them by their parents as legal guardians. Other Issei formed land-holding corporations with 51% of the stock held by American citizens; the legality of such schemes was successfully defended by attorneys Albert Elliott and Guy C. Calden.

(The nature of Japanese farming was to prove a financial boon in the long run. Their small truck-farm acreages became extremely valuable as sites for housing developments and shopping centers as urban centers expanded. Investments in lands that were thought to be worthless also paid off; with reclamation practices, Japanese Americans made productive farms out of what had been wasteland.)

18. A number of Issei and Chinese Americans served in American forces in

World War I in the hope of being
granted citizenship, only to learn
that the promise of citizenship for
service did not apply to "aliens ineligible to citizenship."

19. In 1921 the Japanese government
    stopped female emigration to the
    U.S. because of American hostility to
    their coming.

20. The Cable Act, passed in 1922, pro-
    vided that "any woman citizen who
    marries an alien ineligible to
    citizenship shall cease to be a
    citizen of the United States."

21. The 1924 Immigration Act discrimi-
    nated against immigrants not from
    northern Europe and excluded totally
    "all aliens ineligible to citizen-
    ship."

22. Japanese were denied citizenship by
    the Supreme Court in the Ozawa Case.
    Takeo Ozawa arrived in California
    from Japan in 1884. He graduated
    from high school and then studied

(In 1920, 42.5% of adult male
Japanese Americans were bache-
lors; the effect of anti-
Japanese feeling in America
was to keep many of them in
a state of involuntary celibacy.
It must be remembered that American laws were fairly uniform in
the prohibition of marriages
between Orientals and Whites.)
(The offensive nature of this
legislation led Ambassador
C. E. Woods in Tokyo to resign
in protest. The 1924 Immigration Act may have been the single
most important act--short of
Pearl Harbor itself--which led
to the war between Japan and
the U.S.)

law at the University of California.   (Ozawa died an alien in 1936.

He applied for final citizenship   His only son was killed in

papers on October 16, 1914, asserting   Salerno, Italy, fighting for

that he was free and white. Twenty   the United States.)

years later, the Supreme Court de-

nied him citizenship.

K. Filipinos who had come to the U.S. were   Rabaya, "Filipino Immigration"

experiencing the same kinds of dis-   in Takichi, Wong, Odo and Wong's

crimination and conflict.   Roots: An Asian American Reader

1. Between 1900 and 1910 many Filipinos

came to Hawaii as a result of

economic depression in their home-

land.

2. After World War I, Filipino immigra-   Bulosan, "History of a Moment,"

tion shifted increasingly to the   in Faderman and Bradshaw's

Mainland, with the grestest numbers   Speaking for Ourselves

entering the U.S. between 1920 and

1930.

3. In the Depression, Filipinos were   Bulosan, America is in the Heart

discriminated against by law in much   (There is a relevant excerpt in

the same way that other Asian Ameri-   Haslam's Forgotten Pages of

cans were being discriminated   American Literature.)

against.   Santos, You Lovely People

4. In 1934 Filipino immigration was re-   (Contains a number of stories

stricted to a quota of fifty per   concerning the Filipino ex-

year. Later (in 1946) the quota was   perience in America.)

raised to 100 per year; and in 1965

quotas were abolished.

L. The need for organized efforts to pro-   Hosokawa, "The Birth of JACL,"

tect the rights of Japanese Americans   Nisei: the Quiet Americans

and to lobby against discriminatory

laws became increasingly apparent.

1. In 1918 the American Loyalty League,

a small, loosely-organized group,

was formed to make the way easier for

the Nisei to participate more fully

in American life. This organization

dwindled in the early 1920's.

2. In 1921 the Seattle Progressive Citi-

zens League was formed to combat

anti-Japanese groups, to fight

against discrimination.

3. In 1923 the American Loyalty League

was organized in Fresno. Joining

with other ethnic groups, this Fresno

group successfully sought better com-

munity services to ethnic neighbor-

hoods.

4. The Japanese American Citizens League

was organized in Seattle in 1930.

Having a broader base than the

earlier organizations, JACL was to

prove an effective lobbying power.

a. Suma Sugi of Los Angeles was the   (Suma Sugi was successful in her

first Japanese American lobbyist   lobbying efforts; in 1931 the

when **she** went to Washington, D.C.   Cable Act was amended.)

to work against the injustice of

the Cable Act.

b. Tokutaro Nishimura Slocum, an Issei   (Slocum's campaign, too, was an

veteran of World War I, was chosen   eventual success. Some 700

as lobbyist in the cause of ex-   Issei veterans of World War I

tending citizenship to Issei   gained citizenship.)

veterans of World War I.

c. Mike Masaoka, of Salt Lake City   Masaoka described JACL as

and the University of Utah, was to   ... but a part of the larger
                                       movement through which all
prove an effective leader of JACL   minorities--racial, economic,
                                       political, religious--seek
in World War II and an effective   their just and rightful place
                                       in that heaven of human endeavor
lobbyist.   which must come.

M. World War II brought happier times for

Chinese Americans.

1. The long unfavorable treatment in

America took a favorable direction

when China and the U.S. became allies

in war.

2. Official government propaganda began

to show Chinese in a favorable light;

Chinese Americans came to be seen as fellow humans united in a cause.

3. In 1943 the Chinese Exclusion Act, which had first been passed in 1882, was finally repealed.

N. For Japanese Americans, World War II brought new indignities, with Relocation Camps being the culminating indignity in a long history of injustice.

1. In the years leading up to the war, Americans looked with distrust on Japan as that country's imperialistic aggression increased in Asia.

2. Japanese Americans were harassed in the immediate period in which the war began for America.

   a. Japanese American businesses were closed by federal agents.

   b. The Treasury Department froze bank accounts of Japanese Americans for a time, later easing its restrictions so that Issei and Nisei could draw up to $100 a month for living expenses.

   c. Unfounded rumors of spying and sabotage aroused hostility.

(Repeal of the Chinese Exclusion Act made it possible for families which had been separated by American law to come together at last.)

(Perishable grocery stocks spoiled behind locked doors. Regular customers began to look elsewhere for markets.)

Hosokawa, "The Unhappy Days," Nisei: The Quiet Americans

68

d. The privacy of Japanese American
    citizens was invaded for searches
    without warrants.

e. Issei workers with unblemished
    records of service were fired by
    employers.

f. Business licenses were cancelled;
    even some hospitals refused to
    accept Japanese American patients.

g. In scattered incidents of violence,
    a few Japanese Americans were
    killed; others were injured and
    their possessions destroyed.

h. A number of prominent men began   In reaction to a proposed evacua-
    demanding that Japanese Americans   tion plan presented by California
    be evacuated from the West Coast: Governor Culbert L. Olson, Saburo
    columnists and commentators Damon   Kido, head of JACL (which had
    Runyon, John B. Hughes, Westbrook   become the unofficial voice of
    Pegler, Henry McLemore; Congressman   Japanese Americans), asked,
    Leland Ford, Mayor Fletcher Bowron
    of Los Angeles, Earl Warren (then   Why don't you give us the neces-
    California's attorney general) and   sary police protection so we can
                                             remain in our homes? I consider
    other political figures; Secretary   it the responsibility of the
    of War Henry L. Stimson and some   state to safeguard its citizens.
    military leaders.

i. A plan of evacuation drafted by
Colonel Karl R. Bendetsen was
finally adopted for relocating
Japanese Americans away from the
coastal area.

3. Executive Order 9066, signed by
President F. D. Roosevelt on February
19, 1942, provided for evacuation of
Japanese Americans from many areas of
the West to "relocation centers."
Nearly 25,000 families (117,116 persons in all, nearly two-thirds of
whom were citizens) were uprooted,
leaving behind property worth an
estimated $200 million. After the
war the government repaid at about 30
to 40 cents on the 1942 dollar (with
less valuable post-war dollars), the
last claim being settled in 1965.

Lt. Gen. John L. DeWitt, head
of the Western Defense Command,
stated:

A Jap's a Jap. It makes no
difference whether he is an
American citizen or not. ...
They are a dangerous element,
whether loyal or not.

Yamamoto, "The Legend of Miss
Sasagawara," in Faderman and
Bradshaw's Speaking for Ourselves
(has a relocation camp setting)

4. All persons of Japanese ancestry (defined as one-eighth or more Japanese
blood) were to be excluded from
Military Area Number 1. The evacuation order was somewhat contradictory
in a racist way: "mixed-blood (one-
half Japanese or less) individuals,

Conn, Command Decision

citizens of the United States or of
friendly nations, whose backgrounds
have been Caucasian" were exempted.

5. Japanese Americans were first allowed   (A number who made the voluntary
    to move to the interior of the United   journey to the interior met hos-
    States on a voluntary basis; 8,000   tility **and** threats on the way.)
    voluntarily moved into intermountain
    areas.

6. Strong protests and its own ineffec-
    tiveness brought the termination of
    the voluntary plan.

7. Japanese Americans had a first re-
    action of disbelief because of their
    faith in their Constitutional rights
    as citizens.

9. Reactions of Whites varied:

    a. A number attempted to stop the
        forced exodus through petitions and
        ads in newspapers.

    b. Some offered slights and insults to
        Japanese Americans: anti-Japanese
        feeling began to appear in news-
        papers.

    c. Lack of knowledge of Japanese   (F.B.I. Director J. Edgar Hoover
        Americans caused many to maintain   stated:

negative stereotypes which had been

fostered by adverse writings of

newspaper columnists.

10. On March 22, 1942, Army controlled

    evacuation began. There were two

    stages in the relocation process:

    first to Tanforan and Santa Anita

    race tracks; then to permanent relo-

    cation camps, two in California

    (Manzanar and Tule Lake), two in

    Arizona (Poston and Gila River), and

    one each in Idaho (Minidoka), Wyoming

    (Heart Mountain), Colorado (Granada),

    and Utah (Topaz), and two in Arkansas

    (Rohwer and Jerome).

11. Life in the relocation camps had some

    positive values:

  a. Efficiency of the inmates and their

      sense of community made the opera-

      tion of the relocation centers move

      quite smoothly.

  b. The inmates cooperated to make life

      as pleasant as possible under the

      unpleasant circumstances of the

      camps themselves.

The necessity for mass evacuation is based primarily upon public and political pressure rather than on factual data. Public hysteria and, in some instances, the comments of the press and radio announcers, have resulted in a tremendous amount of pres-sure. ...)

U.S. Department of the Interior,

War Relocation Authority,

Impounded People

Fujimoto, "The Failure of

Democracy in a Time of Crisis"

in Tachiki, Wong, Odo and Wong's

Roots: An Asian American Reader

Bloom and Riemer, Removal and

Return: the Socio-Economic

Effects of the War on Japanese

Americans

c. Japanese Americans were gathered in large groups for the first time, helping them to see around them men of their own race with real abilities in school and genuine creative talents. A sense of pride developed.

d. Schools were run as normally as possible.

Okubo, Citizen 13660

e. Other activities such as Boy Scouting provided interest for youngsters and for some adults who became involved.

f. There was a certain security attached to camp life; for the first time, some had time for relaxation and for concern with things other than making a livelihood.

Kitagawa, Issei and Nisei: the Internment Years

Against the New Year sky,
Beyond the fence flutters
The Stars and Stripes.
   --Haiku by
    Sankuro Nagano

12. There were many negative aspects to camp life.

a. It seemed that there was no way to please some Whites: there were complaints that there was conspicuous waste in the camps; there was resentment that large numbers of

people were not contributing to the
war effort.

b. Armed guards, barbed wire and guard
    towers with machine guns did not
    add to the comfort of the intern-
    ees.

c. Life was monotonous, with nowhere
    to go and little to do.

d. The race track stables and the
    later communal barracks were not
    like home.

e. The family structure was reordered
    because of the lack of privacy,
    the communal duties, and because
    of the dependency on the government
    rather than on the head of the
    household to provide all neces-
    sities.

f. Because of the pattern of depen-
    dency on the government which they
    had become accustomed to, some
    Japanese Americans did not wish to
    leave the centers when the oppor-
    tunity came.

g. Professionals and skilled workers
    (in fact, all) lost the opportunity

Fisher, Exile of a Race

Eaton, Beauty Behind Barbed Wire

Snow upon the rooftop,
Snow upon the coal;
Winter in Wyoming--
Winter in my soul.
        --Miyuki Aoyama

Okubo, "Tanforan," (from

Citizen 13660) in Haslam's

Forgotten Pages of American

Literature

(A surgeon could earn the top

figure--$16 per month for his

74

to gain financially during this

period: wage scales for services

performed by inmates varied from

$8 to $16 per month. Later the pay

was raised to as much as $19 per

month.

13. Milton Eisenhower and Dillon Myer,

who were appointed to the overall

administration of the relocation

camps, were both sympathetic to the

cause of the Nisei, observing the

orderliness and efficiency of Japa-

nese Americans and perceiving that

the large majority were loyal U.S.

citizens.

14. As time went on, inmates of the re-

location camps were given permission

to leave camp if they would go to the

Midwest and to the East.

   a. Several influences brought such a

       move about.

       (1) Nisei servicemen were achieving

            a remarkable military record.

       (2) A number of Japanese Americans

            in the relocation camps were

            providing valuable service as

Study Outline	*Notes and Sources*
workers in surrounding com- munities.	
(3) Civilian administrators were generally in favor of allowing the Nisei citizens their free- dom, as their experience with the Japanese Americans in the camps had impressed them with the loyalty and worthiness of the internees.	Hosokawa, "Behind Barbed Wire," Nisei: The Quiet Americans
b. Many did not wish to leave the camps, for various reasons.	Takahashi, "Nisei, Nisei," in Faderman and Bradshaw's Speaking
(1) A number feared the prejudice and hatred which they felt would be directed toward them were they to leave.	for Ourselves (a poem with the theme of race prejudice)
(2) Some had come to depend on the security of life in the camps.	
(3) Some were resentful at the treatment they had received and did not wish to work for the war effort.	(Most of these were probably not sympathetic to the Japanese cause in the war.)
c. A number left the camps to find work in defense plants and else- where. Like the Nisei soldiers, these workers found prejudice and	(Like the Nisei servicemen, Japanese Americans were not ready to take slanderous statements meekly: at a defense plant, one

76

ill will in some of the men with whom they worked.

15. A number of the inmates of the camps were antagonistic, for a variety of reasons.

   a. While a great majority of the Nisei (second generation, or American born) were loyal citizens, a few of the Issei (born in Japan) were probably sympathetic to Japan rather than the U.S. Some of the Kibei (American born who had been sent to Japan for part of their education) were also loyal to Japan.

   b. The indignities which they had suffered alienated others.

   c. Tule Lake became a segregation camp for those who were disaffected.

   d. On July 1, 1944, Congress passed a special law by which Japanese Americans might renounce their American citizenship. Japanese nationalists were permitted to proselytize other inmates in relocation camps. As a result, 5,371

Japanese American worker--who happened to be the star pitcher on the company ball team--retaliated against a foreman's "dirty Jap"-type remark with a blow to the jaw.)

(See the "Integration versus Nationalism" unit for some details and references relating to a generation and cultural conflict.)

(Hawaiian born Joe Kurihara, who was a World War I veteran, was embittered by the evacuation to the point that he vowed

... to become a Jap a hundred percent and never do another day's work to help this country fight this war.)

(A number of loyal Japanese Americans chose to remain at Tule Lake as well. They became subject to the harassment of nationalist agitators.)

(During the entire war period, 5,766 Nisei renounced their citizenship; 5,409 later asked that it be returned. The

American born citizens signed
applications renouncing their
citizenship. A few of these were
later removed to Japan to become
Japanese citizens.

e. War Relocation Authority efforts
to establish criteria for segregation were inept as well as im-
practical.

(1) The same questionnaire which had
been used to screen male Nisei
of draft age for military service and for work in defense in-
dustries was submitted to Issei
and to women.

(2) Questions 27 and 28 were sup-
posed to be answered "yes," but
they proved difficult for many.

(a) Question 27 asked,

Are you willing to serve in
the armed forces of the United
States on combat duty, when-
ever ordered?

(b) Question 28 asked,

Will you swear unqualified
allegiance to the United
States of America and faith-
fully defend the United States
from any or all attack by

renunciation was voided by the
U.S. District Court in San
Francisco after five years of
litigation.)

(Women and Issei--many of whom
were quite old--did not wish to
volunteer for combat: presumably
they were disloyal.)
An affirmative answer by Issei
would make them stateless per-
sons--they could not become U.S.

domestic forces, and foreswear any form of allegiance of obedience to the Japanese emperor, to any other foreign government, power or organization?	citizens--so they did not respond affirmatively.

(c)   Even the Nisei had experienced some confusion over these questions. Some answered "no" to the two questions out of resentment at the discriminatory treatment they had received. Some gave conditional responses, "Yes, if my rights as a citizen are restored." Some felt that to "foreswear" allegiance to Japan would be to admit that such allegiance had existed.

Okada, No-No Boy (The No-No boys were considered disloyal in the statistical analysis of the responses.)

(d)   The questionnaire was changed after officials in administration came to understand what they themselves had been asking.

16. In the meantime the JACL with wartime headquarters in Salt Lake City under the direction of Mike Masaoka was lobbying for fair treatment for Japanese Americans.

Hosokawa, "The Dedicated JACL-ERS," Nisei: The Quiet Americans

Study Outline	*Notes and Sources*

a. Masaoka and the JACL won the support of seventy widely known respected men and women "sponsors."

b. An unofficial and informal advisory
committee assisted Masaoka: Roger
W. Baldwin of the American Civil
Liberties Union, the writer Pearl
Buck, Reed Lewis of the Common
Council for American Unity, Norman
Thomas of the Post War World
Council, Dr. John W. Thomas of the
American Baptist Home Missions
Council, Annie Clo Watson of the
San Francisco International Insti-
tute and the Young Women's Chris-
tian Association, Clarence Pickett
of the American Friends Service
Committee and Masaoka's friends in
Congress, especially the Utah
Senators Thomas and Murdock.

(Senator Elbert Thomas had been
a Mormon missionary to Japan
and had later taught at University of Utah--where Masaoka was
a brilliant student under him.)

c. With the aid of these influential
people, Masaoka and the JACL were
successful in a number of lobbying
projects.

17. The Pacific Citizen, first published
in San Francisco and later in

(Masaoka himself volunteered for
service with the 442nd when the
opportunity presented itself.
He was to return later to continue his successful career as a
lobbyist after the war ended.)

80

Seattle, became the editorial voice
of the Nisei in World War II when it
was published in Salt Lake City under
the editorship of Larry Tajiri.

O. After World War II there remained much
to be done in the struggle for the
rights of Asian Americans.

  1. In 1950 there were still more than
500 federal, state and local laws and
ordinances aimed directly or in-
directly against resident Japanese
Americans. (The 1924 Immigration
Law was still in effect, at least for
Japanese. And Issei were still not
eligible for citizenship.)

Hayakawa, "Communication: Inter-
racial and International," in
Haslam's Forgotten Pages of
American Literature
(This essay deals with communication in the struggle for civil
rights.)

  2. Japanese Americans had lost most of
their property due to relocation;
there was the problem of reparations.

  3. Saburo Kido, pre-war JACL leader who
had been interned with his family,
recruited Mike Masaoka to return to
his lobbying efforts instead of to
newspaper work as he had intended.

(Masaoka had offers from the
New York Times and from the New
York World-Telegram.)

  4. In 1946 lobbying efforts were aimed
at getting naturalization rights for

Issei. Kido also announced the goal
of revision of the 1924 immigration
law which discriminated against
Asians.

5. Masaoka began a rather quiet lobbying
   campaign which eventually gained some
   support: Congressman Walter Judd of
   Minnesota, a onetime medical missionary in China, became interested;
   and Congressman Ed Gossett of Texas,
   who remembered the 442nd's rescue of
   the Lost Battalion of the Texas Division, heard Masaoka and became a
   strong advocate of liberalizing the
   immigration laws.

6. On July 2, 1948, President Truman   (This act provided for payment
   signed the Japanese American Evacua-   for claims of property lost
   tion Claims Act.   through relocation.)

7. Through an amendment to the Soldier
   Brides Bill, Japanese spouses and
   children of American servicemen were
   permitted to enter the U.S. without
   regard to the Oriental Exclusion Act.

8. California, meantime, was confis-
   cating Japanese American property,
   claiming that land had been purchased

82

"with intent to violate and evade the alien land law." In the Oyama case the San Diego Superior Court ruled in favor of the state; on appeal, the California Supreme Court upheld that decision, ruling that the state could exclude ineligible aliens from any interest in agricultural lands; the U.S. Supreme Court ruled in Oyama's favor, stating in its decision the obvious fact that "the only basis for this discrimination against an American citizen ... was the fact that his father was Japanese. ..." (Oyama had purchased land in his son's name.) The escheat action itself was declared unconstitutional.

9. Other cases followed which firmly established the unconstitutionality of California's alien land law. In the Fujii case, in which the state sought to escheat a city lot purchased by an Issei businessman, the District Court ruled the alien land law "untenable and unenforceable" because it violated the United Nations Charter. In

(Following this legal victory in the Oyama case, the JACL helped persuade the California legislature to appropriate funds to reimburse those whose land had been escheated.)

83

Masaoka v. California an effort was made to show that the alien land law abridged the rights of American citizens of Japanese ancestry. In this test case, five citizen sons transferred title to an unimproved city lot to their Issei mother. Under the alien land law this gift was illegal.

Under the law the giving of this gift would make the five sons felons. (The successful court action was dramatized by the fact that four of the sons were combat veterans and a fifth had been killed in the rescue of the Lost Battalion.) The decision in the Masaoka case found the alien land law itself unconstitutional.

10. California had denied commercial fishing licenses to Issei ("aliens ineligible to citizenship"). In Takahashi v. Fish and Game Commission, the Supreme Court upheld the rights of Issei to engage in commercial fishing.

11. In 1950 Congressman Walter H. Judd introduced a measure to authorize the naturalization of any qualified alien without respect to race or national origin.

(The House passed this resolution unanimously, but Senate amendments to the measure caused President Truman to veto it.)

12. The Walter-McCarran Immigration and Naturalization Act of 1952 (introduced by Senator Pat McCarran of Nevada and Congressman Francis E. Walter of Pennsylvania) was finally

passed after much lobbying by Mike

Masaoka and other Nisei veterans.

13. Shortcomings of the Walter-McCarran
    Act (immigration quotas continued to
    be heavily weighted in favor of north
    Europeans) were eliminated in a new
    immigration bill signed by President
    Lyndon B. Johnson in 1965.

14. In 1968 a National JACL Committee to
    Repeal the Emergency Detention Act
    (Title II of the Internal Security
    Act) was formed. Remembering their
    own experiences, Japanese Americans
    see in Title II (which provides for
    detection camps) and Title I (di-
    rected at controlling subversive
    activities) dangerous laws which
    might be used in unjust and discrimi-
    natory ways to establish "concentra-
    tion camps," or to harass American
    people.

(Under the 1965 law, 340,000
immigrants are permitted to
enter the U.S. annually on a
basis of skills and relationship to those already here and
not on the basis of race, creed
or nationality.)

Kitagawa, "Epilogue from Issei
and Nisei," in Haslam's Forgotten Pages of American
Literature and in Kitagawa's
book (presents arguments against
segregation)

Odo, Uyematsu, Hanada, Li and
Chung, "The U.S. in Asia and Asians
in America" in Tachiki, Wong, Odo
and Wong's Roots

III   Conclusion

By and large, it was not the cultural differences of Chinese and Japanese
immigrants which formed the basis of conflict between the Asian American and
Whites in America. True, Oriental cultures were different in some ways from
European cultures and from the American traditions which are derived from them.

Such differences seemed quaint, or odd--or even suspicious--to some Americans; they were causes of some degree of conflict.

But simple conformity to American styles or adoption of American ways did not end discrimination by Whites nor the conflicts which were generated by that discrimination. When the Chinese immigrant cut off his queue in 1911 after the overthrow of the Manchus in China, there was hardly a perceptible change in American attitudes toward him. In fact, discriminatory laws against Chinese were to continue to become even more oppressive for some time after that event.

When Nisei testified before Congressional committees and elsewhere, official America was surprised to find that most second-generation Japanese Americans were much like other Americans in habits and beliefs: only a small percentage understood the Japanese language (such a small number were fluent in Japanese that the Army spent a good deal of time and money training the less fluent Nisei so that it could have sufficient interpreters to use in Military Intelligence assignments); few had more than a rudimentary knowledge of Japanese history or philosophy. These facts surprised those who had believed the slogan "A Jap is a Jap," so much so that some officials found such testimony unbelievable. White Americans could see with their very eyes that the Nisei were different.

Asian Americans tried to achieve a share of America's bounty by middle-class-conformity, living exemplary lives of industry and efficiency. There was much in the ethical and practical cultural backgrounds of most Asian immigrants which corresponded to middle class American standards of ethics and behavior. And in America, there were official ideals (contained in important legal documents such as the Constitution) of equal justice, the right to own property, freedom of conscience--which the immigrant and his citizen children found very desirable.

But the Asian American looked different. And many Americans were ready to take up their part of the "white man's burden" by discriminating against Asian Americans. Some politicians and labor leaders made a living, a career, out of fanning the flames of race hate.

For the Asian immigrant, life was a struggle for bread and a struggle for justice. Tactics used in the struggle varied from relative passivity and acceptance of injustice, to banding together for protection and fellowship and justice.

Thoughtful individuals found ways of getting around laws whose intent was to keep the Asian American in poverty and in a subordinate social and political position in America.

Chinese and Japanese governments used diplomatic pressures to aid their citizens in the fight against injustice in America.

World War II brought changes to the conflict scene. The Chinese image or identity assumed positive characteristics (with the result that after the war the great majority of Chinese immigrants were young women, often with small children, who had come to America to be with their men--after long years of separation due to American laws). Japanese Americans, on the other hand, became the objects of increased hostility and increasingly repressive and unjust official measures.

The patriotic display of selfless bravery made by Nisei servicemen (a tour de force, if the pun could be forgiven) so impressed the nation that it could only capitulate to claims for justice for the brave men who had served so well--and for the families which had produced them.

America had a lot on its collective conscience. And Mike Masaoka and others (Masaoka had served in the 442nd as its public relations officer) were not ready to let Americans forget it. Lobbying and using court action to secure justice, the Nisei made solid progress.

Other forces were working to good effect to secure greater justice and equal opportunity for all. The Blacks in their struggle for civil rights were at the same time helping the cause of Asian Americans.

Though much was accomplished in the cause of human rights in the post-war years, there had been injustices which were impossible to right. Some American citizens had left the country never to return. Others were to feel strongly the need to speak out against injustice, so that the American dreams should not again turn to nightmare.

The tide of immigration has turned. Asian groups are dominating today's influx. Some young Asian Americans, mistrustful of the American system, are asking for an increased Asian American solidarity and for a third world alliance of "have nots" (of whatever racial origin) against the "haves" of the world.

PART THREE: INTEGRATION VERSUS NATIONALISM--
ASIAN AMERICAN DILEMMA

I   Introduction

Most American immigrants from the Orient had strong nationalistic
leanings. With the tenacity of overseas Chinese everywhere, Chinese Americans maintained cultural and family ties in the land of their ancestors, sup-
porting parents and wives and children who remained behind. The early
immigrant fully expected to return to the village of his birth once he had
provided for security in retirement.

Japanese immigrants retained ties to their homeland, and in return received support from the Japanese government.

American immigration laws had the effect of strengthening these cultural
ties to the land of birth, at the same time preventing the maintenance of
close family relationships between American-based fathers and their Oriental
wives and children.

First generation Asian Americans (like other ethnic groups) were drawn
together because of common language and customs. Violence and racial discrimination (which was often channeled through law) reinforced the nationalistic
tendency to maintain cultural identity and made segregation necessary for protection and self-interest, even for those who had mastered American language
and customs.

Of the later generations, many did not acquire strong cultural ties with
the countries of their fathers. Instead, they took the course of cultural
assimilation. Even so, most of their desires for complete integration were
thwarted by prejudice, or by law until very recent years.

Young Asian Americans are less patient than their fathers. Singling out
Asian Americans for discrimination (Chinese Exclusion or Japanese American
relocation) bred resentments which find expression among today's young
militants.

A number of identifiable organizations or groups developed to represent
aspects of the contrasting impulses to nationalism or integration. Among
Chinese Americans the following associations, groups or organizations represent in one way or another the nationalistic trend: the Chinatowns, the
fongs (local organizations), family associations (with larger membership
and broader functions than the fongs) and the Chinese Benevolent Association
(the Chinese Six Companies of San Francisco was the first such organization),
and the lodges and tongs (which were transplanted from China originally,
bringing with them some of the quarrels and conflicts of rival Chinese fac-
tions). The Chinese American Citizens Alliance, which was organized by young
American-born citizens, is probably the most notable integrationist organization.

Among the Japanese Americans, the most obvious nationalistic movement developed among disgruntled <u>Issei</u> and <u>Kibei</u> in World War II relocation camps. In contrast, the dominant integrationist organization has been the Japanese American Citizens League, which was organized in 1930. A number of other earlier integrationist groups had been formed, some to die out and some to join JACL (which has been derisively called "jackal" by some militants with nationalistic or third world leanings).

The present status of Asian Americans lies somewhere between the poles of nationalism and integration. Most young Asian Americans have assimilated the middle class cultural values of America, but they are part of a society which is closer to pluralism than to complete integration.

II   Guide and Sourcebook

Study Outline	*Notes and Sources*
A. Early Chinese Americans held tenaciously to their cultural identity and to the hope of return to China for retirement, reunion with family and for death.	
1. Cultural ties and philosophical and religious beliefs prompted Chinese emigrants to band together wherever they settled.	Mitchison, <u>The Overseas Chinese</u>
2. The language barrier was an incentive to the first Chinese Americans to join together.	
3. Loyalty of American Chinese to their Chinese homeland and their families was reflected in their financial support of families (parents, wives and children), and community institutions such as schools in their home	Mark Twain, <u>Roughing It</u> (Twain describes Virginia City, Nevada's Chinese section, customs such as sending the dead back to China for burial and some quaint schemes of Whites to discourage immigration.)

villages in China. (The Toishan area in China became prosperous due to remittances sent home by Chinese in America and elsewhere.)

4. Evidence of the close ties of Chinese Americans to the Chinese homeland is found in the fact that they wore the queue, or pigtail, which was a symbol of bondage, until 1911 when the Manchu dynasty lost its control in China. Only then did Chinese Americans cut off their long hair, even though the queues had been marks of "otherness" and, therefore, cause of ridicule in America.

B. White aggression and prejudicial law intensified nationalistic feelings of Chinese Americans.

1. Chinese who regarded the Middle King-   Mitchison, The Overseas Chinese
   dom as the best culture and all others as inferior probably found confirmation for their tradition that all outside the Middle Kingdom were barbarians when Whites used violence for seemingly inexplicable reasons.

2. Retreating from competition as
   laborers, Chinese Americans formed
   communities of their own to provide
   the security which was denied them
   elsewhere.

3. Traditional family business patterns
   were used; kinsmen were given job
   preference.

4. Lodges and tongs provided fellowship
   for men who had no wives or children.
   (Tongs also kept alive old rivalries.)

5. The Chinese government did not look
   with favor on the discrimination her
   citizens faced abroad. To support
   citizens abroad, in 1909 the Ching
   court of China passed an edict recog-
   nizing the children of Chinese
   fathers as Chinese wherever they were
   born.

6. The Six Companies became a strong in-   Sung, Mountain of Gold (Betty
   fluence over the Chinese Americans in   Sung describes Chinatown:
   San Francisco. When justice was de-   An invisible moat seemed to cut
   nied them through the usual court   the Chinese off from the main-
                                               stream of American life just be-
   channels, Chinese Americans set up   yond the borders. From birth to
                                               death, a Chinese found his needs

91

what amounted to a completely sepa-

rate system. Betty Sung says,

As the Chinese tried to side-step
or avoid all contact with American
government agencies, they formed
their own organizations to provide
some form of quasi-government that
would set up rules and regulations,
resolve differences between them,
care for the needy and infirm, and
act as liaison with the outside.
(Mountain of Gold, 134)

7.   The Six Companies performed a number   Hoy, The Chinese Six Companies

of services for Chinese Americans,

exacting in return loyalty and sub-

mission to its leadership.

8.   The tongs also provided fraternity   Glick and Sheng-Hwa, Swords of

and services to members, including   Silence: Chinese Secret

the hui which served as a banking   Societies, Past and Present

institution. Tong rivalries and, for

a time, engagement in protection

rackets were to add to the image of

the Chinese American. (Later, tongs

reverted to their role of social

lodges; although a few tong leaders

retained a great deal of influence

in the Chinatowns.)

9.   The Chinese Benevolent Associations

(successors to the Six Companies and

other such organizations) maintained

*met within the enclave of an
area ten blocks square. He
lived a way of life as his parent
remembered it back in the villages
of Kwangtung Province.)*

the nationalistic leadership of
Chinese America well into the 20th
Century.

10. Chinese language publications were
    also a part of Chinese American
    separatism. (There were eleven
    Chinese language newspapers in the
    U.S. in 1967.)

11. Chinese American nationalism which
    identified with the Chinese homeland
    was adversely affected by the 1937
    invasion of South China by Japan and
    by the later domination of China by
    a Communist government which threat-
    ened traditional Chinese society and
    culture. Overseas dependents, who
    generally lived more prosperously
    than their neighbors, did not fare
    well under the new Communist govern-
    ment.

C. Leadership in the fight for the integrationist cause of equal rights and
   equal justice--in business, labor,
   politics and social life--developed
   among young Chinese American citizens.

1. In 1904 a group of native-born sons
   rejected the leadership of the
   Chinese Six Companies to form the
   Native Sons of the Golden State, with
   the design of helping the American-
   born to participate in all phases of
   American life. Walter U. Lum, Joseph
   K. Lum, and Ng Gunn were the founders
   of this first integrationist group
   dedicated to defending and securing
   the rights of Chinese American citizens.

2. Such a movement was obviously a re-   Lee Yu-Hwa, "The Last Rite,"
   flection of a generation gap and a   Speaking for Ourselves
   cultural gap as well. First genera-   Buck, "The Old Mother," "The
   tion Chinese Americans were finding   New Road," and Hearts Come Home,"
   their children estranged from them   in Hearts Come Home and Other
   and from the customs and culture of   Stories (Some of these stories
   the China which they had remembered.   have Chinese settings.)

3. Soon other chapters of Native Sons of   Sung, Mountain of Gold
   the Golden State were formed.
   Chinese Americans in other states
   expressed a desire to form chapters.
   When the organization became national
   in scope, the name was changed to
   Chinese American Citizens Alliance.

(Membership in CACA is by invitation; membership is considered a recognition of achievement as well as ability and a willingness to work for the advancement of Chinese Americans.)

D. Japanese Americans had nationalistic leanings similar in many ways to those of Chinese Americans.

1. First generation Japanese Americans (_Issei_) retained their Japanese citizenship and were given political and diplomatic support of the Japanese government.

2. Cultural ties and a common language were strong incentives for working and settling together. Communities of Japanese Americans developed, the largest in Los Angeles.

Mori, _Yokahama, California_

3. Japanese Americans created their own businesses (usually family-centered like those of Chinese Americans) when they were discriminated against in the labor market.

| *Study Outline* | *Notes and Sources* |

4. Japanese language schools were established to teach Japanese language and
culture.

Sone, Nisei Daughter

5. There were a number of other evi-
dences of a cultural separatism which
might be interpreted as being at
least in some ways and to some degree
nationalistic in character: Japanese
language publications (including
newspapers such as the Nichi Bei);
athletic leagues; acting groups; and
the Tachibana-Haiku Society for
example.

6. A number of second generation (Nisei)
sons were sent to Japan for part of
their education. (The Nisei who were
educated in Japan were called Kibei;
they often felt more inclination to
the traditional Japan-oriented
nationalism than other Nisei, who
were becoming like other Americans in
their habits and desires.)

Hosokawa, Nisei: the Quiet
Americans
(See Pat Sumi's account of her
own reaction to a recent visit
to Japan, in "An Interview with
Pat Sumi" in Tachiki, Wong, Odo,
and Wong's Roots: An Asian
American Reader.)
Kitagawa, Issei and Nisei: the
Internment Years

7. The last dramatic nationalistic movement which was oriented toward Japan
was probably due as much to reaction

(See also the "Conflict" unit for
other details and references.)

to repression and restrictions im-
posed on Japanese Americans in World
War II as it was to a simple
nationalistic impulse. Joe Kurihara
and other disgruntled <u>Issei</u> led a
strongly nationalistic movement in
the relocation camps. (That this
movement was strongly motivated by
unpleasant conditions of the times
rather than by a basic loyalty to
Japan is born out by the fact that
of the 5,766 <u>Nisei</u> who renounced
their U.S. citizenship during the
entire period of war, 5,409 later
asked that it be returned.)

E. Citizen-born Japanese Americans were   "Autobiography of a Sansei Female,"
    unwilling to accept the separatism   in Tachiki, Wong, Odo and Wong's
    which their parents had lived with.   <u>Roots: An Asian American Reader</u>
    They began to ask for integration and   (reflects mixed feelings of a
    a full participation in American life.   young Japanese American woman
                                               who is married to a white, about
1. In 1918 The American Loyalty League,   her own experiences and desires)
    the short-lived pioneer integra-
    tionist organization, was formed.

2. In 1930, the Japanese American Citi-   Hosokawa, "The Birth of JACL,"
    zens League was organized. This was   <u>Nisei: the Quiet Americans</u>
    the first integrationist organization   (See also the "Conflict" unit for

97

Study Outline	Notes and Sources

to include a broader than local base.
(There had been several local organizations with similar objectives
before JACL.) JACL was to become the
dominant organization in the Japanese
American cause of integration. A
number of leaders with real ability
were able to achieve important objectives in the integrationist cause.
(Saburo Kido, Mike Masaoka, and other
JACL leaders used persuasion and
quiet but persistent lobbying efforts
to win support for their cause.)

details.)

(See the "Identity" unit for
other important men in the
civil rights movement.)
Takahashi, "The Widower," in
Faderman and Bradshaw's
Speaking for Ourselves

3. The change from acceptance of America's separated society to insistence
upon equal rights and opportunities
represented a growing cultural gap
between immigrants and their children.

Lin Yutang, Chinatown Family
(Reveals some of the effects
of the cultural gap)

4. The immigrants themselves had done
much to achieve a base from which
their children could ask for equality
with justification.

Petersen, "Success Story,
Japanese American Style," in
Kurokawa's Minority Responses

  a. Their habits of hard work conformed
     to the American middle class
     values.

Study Outline	*Notes and Sources*

b. For the most part, Asian Americans have been exemplary in abiding by the law. Strong family ties discouraged juvenile delinquency; it was considered a disgrace to the family for a youngster to be apprehended by the police for law-breaking.

c. A number of Japanese Americans joined Christian (usually Protestant) churches. Mike Masaoka, who may be the most successful of all Asian American lobbyists, is a Mormon (a fact which may have been helpful in getting Utah's anti-miscegenation laws removed from the books). Early Japanese Christians in America were often segregated by such means as being sent to "Chinese" congregations by white church officials.

d. Young Asian Americans availed themselves of educational opportunities, surpassing other groups (including Whites) on an average, in terms of number of years of school completed.

Okimoto, American in Disguise (Daniel Okimoto notes that "Acculturation has resulted in the erosion of some of the principle qualities that set Japanese apart as a particularly law-abiding minority.")

See also Stanford Lyman's "Red Guard on Grant Avenue," Viewpoints (Lyman points to a similar phenomenon among Chinese American youth, and to the rise of organized protests against poverty and neglect in San Francisco's Chinatown.)

(Buddhism and other Oriental religions, with the possible exception of a few nationalistic tenets of Shinto, were not in themselves hindrances to integration, excepting in the preachings and beliefs of some Christians.)

(See the "Conflict" unit for some details.)

Study Outline	Notes and Sources

e. Much of the writing of Asian Americans in recent years has been meliorative and integrationist in tone.

E. Though it has not received the attention of the Black Power movement and recent black nationalist groups, there has developed in the last few years a new Asian American nationalism with Third World leanings.

1. The new nationalists no longer look to Japan or to China; instead they urge a unity of all Asian Americans.

2. Third World nationalism seeks a coalition of all who are discriminated against, a coalition of all the world's "have nots" against the "haves" who oppress them.

3. The Asian American Political Alliances, Asian Americans for Action and Asian American Student Associations, and other groups have formed to express concern about injustice, racism, and repression.

(Hosokawa's Nisei: the Quiet Americans and Sung's Mountain of Gold are generally integrationist in tone, as are Hayakawa's statements in An Interview with S. I. Hayakawa in Tachiki, Wong, Odo and Wong, Roots: An Asian American Reader)

Rev. Lloyd K. Wake, "Shhh! An Asian American Speaking," Hokubei Mainichi (In this sermon which advocates militancy, Rev. Wake takes to task the book Nisei: the Quiet Americans.)

Lyman, "Red Guard on Grant Avenue," in Viewpoints

Uyematsu "The Emergence of Yellow Power in America," and Okimoto, "The Intolerance of Success," in Tachiki, Wong, Odo and Wong's Roots: An Asian American Reader

Tom Englehardt, "Ambush at Kamikaze Pass,"

Bulletin of Concerned Asian Scholars, III (Winter-Spring 1971),

Study Outline	*Notes and Sources*

4. In 1969 J.U.S.T. (Japanese Americans United in Their Search for Truth) was formed to successfully protest the dismissal without hearing of Dr. Thomas Noguchi as Chief Medical Examiner-Coroner of Los Angeles.

64-84.

(Several selections in Roots: An Asian American Reader reflect recent militant and Third World viewpoints.)

5. A number of Young Asian American writers reflect in their writings their discontent with racism, repression and injustice.

III Conclusion

The history of the Asian American in the United States covers a much shorter span of time than that of the Indian (whose American origins are not really clear to us, but which we learn of metaphorically through myths, and which we speculate about in a hundred theories, a number of which may be correct). The span of Asian American history is shorter, too, than that of the Chicano, the Black or the White in what is now the United States. Of these five groups, the Asian American is alone in that his history in what is now the United States began after the United States became a sovereign nation.

The black man was purposely stripped of his own cultural background and, following his slavery, placed in a rather odd position in relation to the white man's laws. The two chief offenses for which he might suffer punishment were (1) acting like a white man, and (2) not acting like a white man.

Oriental Americans, on the other hand, had their own strong cultural identities to serve as bases on which to remain or from which to move into the cultural mainstream.

The law relating to Asian Americans was often as discriminatory as that relating to Blacks. Perhaps it was less ambiguous, less confusing, because it was more evenly administered from place to place. There was no "North" for the Asian American to escape to.

The course of Asian American nationalism lacked the dramatic quality of Garvey's back-to-Africa movement or the later dynamics of Malcolm X. But Asian American unity was based on a cultural, social and, partially, economic separatism which was in itself a type of nationalism.

The nationalism of first generation Asian Americans was often a matter of practical necessity; the 19th Century temper of America was mixed certainly, but it had a strong element of racial intolerance which made the failure of attempts at integration a foregone conclusion.

In twentieth century America, the tradition of intolerance remained. But citizen sons of immigrant fathers had been to American schools (segregated though some of them were) and had been impressed by the guarantees of the Constitution. Having had less firsthand experience with violence and racism, they were perhaps less cynical about the possibilities of those promises being fulfilled.

Organizing their efforts, they told the Asian American story (in which they were out-middle-classing the middle class) of Asian American loyalty, achievement and general good citizenship. Later, many gave their lives for a chance at integration and the American dream, shaming America into legal concessions toward integrationist goals (after the American conscience was pricked by Asian American lobbyists working for just laws).

Much of the writing of Asian Americans of recent years has been integrationist in tone (though it has certainly pointed out injustice). There is a growing Third World movement which is reflected increasingly in print. The Third World exponents call for a new nationalism based on stronger ties among all Asian Americans (forgetting the old divisions based on ancestral country) and a coalition of all "have nots" regardless of race against the "haves" of the world.

Asian-American Bibliography

American Academy of Political and Social Science. Chinese and Japanese in America. San Francisco: R & E, 1970.

Anderson, David D., and Robert L. Wright, editors. The Dark and Tangled Path. Boston: Houghton Mifflin, 1971.

Barth, Gunther. Bitter Strength. Cambridge: Harvard, 1964.

Battistini, Lawrence H. Japan and America. Westport, Connecticut: Greenwood, 1970.

Beach, D. C. Oriental Crime in California. Stanford: Stanford University, 1932.

Beardsley, R. K., J. W. Hall and R. E. Ward. Village Japan. Chicago: University of Chicago, 1959.

Bell, Richard. Public School Education of Second-Generation Japanese in California. Stanford University Series in Education-Psychology, Vol. 3, 1935.

Benedict, Ruth. The Chrysanthemum and the Sword. New York: World, 1967.

Bloom, Leonard, and John Kitsuse. The Managed Casualty. Berkeley: University of California, 1956.

_____, and Ruth Riemer. Removal and Return: The Socio-Economic Effects of the War on Japanese Americans. Berkeley: University of California, 1949.

Blyth, R. H. Haiku. (4 vols.) Japan: Hokuseido, 1950.

Boddy, Elias M. Japanese in America. San Francisco: R & E, 1970.

Bosworth, Allan R. America's Concentration Camps. New York: W. W. Norton and Co., 1967.

Bownas, Geoffrey, and Anthony Thwaite, editors and translators. The Penquin Book of Japanese Verse. Baltimore: Penguin Books, 1968.

Buck, Pearl S. Fairy Tales of the Orient. New York: Simon and Schuster, 1965.

_____. The Good Earth. New York: Pocket Books, 1968.

_____. Hearts Come Home and Other Stories. New York: Pocket Books, 1970.

Bulosan, Carlos. America Is in the Heart. New York: Harcourt, Brace, 1946.

Bureau of Sociological Research, Colorado River War Relocation Center. "The Japanese Family in America," Annals of the American Academy of Political and Social Science. September, 1943.

Burma, John. "Current Leadership Problems Among Japanese-Americans," Sociological and Social Research, XXXVII (1953), 157-163.

California State Board of Control. California and the Oriental. San Francisco: R & E, 1970.

Caudill, William, and George DeVos. "Achievement, Culture and Personality: The Case of the Japanese Americans," American Anthropologist, December 1956.

Chang, Diana. The Frontiers of Love. New York: Random House, 1956.

_____. A Passion for Life. New York: Random House, 1961.

_____. A Woman of Thirty. New York: Random House, 1959.

Chang, M. Tides from the West. New Haven: Yale University, 1947.

Chen, Theodore H. E. "The Oriental-American's Plight." Los Angeles Times, June 8, 1969.

"Chinese Riot and Massacre of September 2, 1885," History of the Union Pacific Coal Mines 1868 to 1940. Omaha: Colonial Press, no date.

Chu, Daniel, and Samuel Chu. Passage to the Golden Gate. New York: Zenith Books, 1967.

Chu, Louis. Eat a Bowl of Tea. New York: Lyle Stuart, 1961.

Chuang, Hua. Crossings. New York: Dial, 1969.

Cleland, R. G. A History of California, The American Period. New York: Macmillan, 1922.

Collidge, M. Chinese Immigration. New York: Henry Holt, 1909.

Conn, Stetson. Command Decision. Washington, D.C.: Office of Military History, U.S. Department of the Army, 1960.

Crow, Carl. Four Hundred Million Customers. London: Hamish Hamilton, 1937.

Culin, Stewart. The I Hing or Patriotic Rising. San Francisco: R & E, 1970.

Daniels, Roger. The Politics of Prejudice. New York: Atheneum, 1968.

_____. Concentration Camps U.S.A. New York: Holt, Rinehart and Winston, 1971.

_____, and Harry H. L. Kitano. American Racism. Englewood Cliffs, New
    Jersey: Prentice Hall, 1970.

Davis, Albert R., editor. The Penguin Book of Chinese Verse. Baltimore:
    Penguin, 1962.

DeVos, George, and Hiroshi Wagatsuma. Japan's Invisible Race. Berkeley:
    University of California, 1966.

Dillon, Richard H. The Hatchet Men. New York: Coward-McCann, 1962.

Divine, Robert A. American Immigration Policy, 1924-1952. New York:
    Plenum, 1971.

Eaton, Allen. Beauty Behind Barbed Wire. New York: Harper, 1953.

Elegant, Robert A. The Dragon's Seed. New York: St. Martin's, 1959.

Elsinore, Sister M. Alfreda. Idaho Chinese Lore. Cottonwood, Idaho:
    Benedictine Sisters, 1971.

Englehart, Tom. "Ambush at Kamikaze Pass." Bulletin of Concerned Asian
    Scholars, III (Winter-Spring 1971), pp. 64-84.

Erickson, Al. "L.A.'s Nisei Today," California Sun Magazine, Summer 1958.

Faderman, Lillian, and Barbara Bradshaw, editors. Speaking for Ourselves.
    Glenview, Illinois: Scott, Foresman, 1969.

Fisher, Anne M. Exile of a Race. Seattle: F. & T. Publishers, 1965.

Girdner, Audrie, and Anne Loftis. The Great Betrayal: The Evacuation of the
    Japanese-Americans During World War II. New York: Macmillan, 1969.

Glick, Carl. Double Ten. New York: McGraw Hill, 1941.

_____. Shake Hands with the Dragon. New York: McGraw Hill, 1941.

_____. Three Times I Bow. New York: Whittlesley House, 1943.

_____, and Hon Sheng-Hwa. Swords of Silence: Chinese Secret Societies,
    Past and Present. New York: Whittlesley House, 1947.

Goldberg, George. East Meets West. New York: Harcourt Brace Jovanovich, 1970.

Gonzalez, N. V. M. Selected Stories. Denver: Swallow Press, 1964.

Gordzins, M. Americans Betrayed. Chicago: University of Chicago, 1949.

Griswold, Wesley S. A Work of Giants. New York: McGraw Hill, 1962.

Gulick, S. L. The American Japanese Problem. New York: Scribner's, 1914.

Hansen, Gladys C., compiler. <u>The Chinese in California</u>. Portland, Oregon: Richard Abel, 1970.

Harada, Tasuku, editor. <u>The Japanese Problem in California</u>. San Francisco: R & E, 1971.

Haslam, Gerald W., editor. <u>Forgotten Pages of American Literature</u>. Boston: Houghton Mifflin, 1970.

Holbrook, Stewart. <u>The Story of American Railroads</u>. New York: Crown, 1947.

Hosokawa, Bill. <u>NISEI The Quiet Americans</u>. New York: William Morrow, 1969.

Hoy, William. <u>The Chinese Six Companies</u>. San Francisco: California Chinese Historical Society, 1942.

Hsiung, S. I. <u>Lady Precious Stream</u>. New York: Samuel French, 1962.

Hsu, Francis L. K. <u>Americans and Chinese: Two Ways of Life</u>. New York: Henry Schumann, 1953.

_____. <u>Under the Ancestors' Shadow</u>. London: Routledge and Kegan Paul, 1949.

Hsu, Kai-yu, and Helen Palubinskas, editors. <u>Asian-American Authors</u>. Boston: Houghton Mifflin, 1972.

Ichihashi, Yamato. <u>Japanese Immigration</u>. San Francisco: R & E, 1970.

_____. <u>Japanese in the United States</u>. New York: Arno Press and New York Times, 1969.

Inada, Lawson. <u>Before the War: Poems as they Happened</u>. New York: William Morrow, 1971.

Inouye, Daniel K. <u>Journey to Washington</u>. Englewood Cliffs: Prentice Hall, 1967.

Irwin, Will. <u>Old Chinatown</u>. New York: Mitchell Kennerley, 1908.

Iwata, Masakazu. "The Japanese Immigrants in California Agriculture," <u>Agricultural History</u>. XXXVI (1962), 25-37.

Johnson, Herbert B. <u>Discrimination Against the Japanese in California</u>. San Francisco: R & E, 1971.

<u>Kabuki Plays</u>: "Kanjincho" and "The Zen Substitute." Adapted by James R. Brandon and Tamako Niwa. New York: Samuel French, 1966.

Kaneko, Hisakazu. <u>Manjiro, The Man Who Discovered America</u>. Boston: Houghton Mifflin, 1956.

Kao-Tong-Kia. Lute Song. Adapted by Will Irwin and Sidney Howard. Chicago: Dramatic Publishing, 1954.

Kelsey, Carl, editor. Present-Day Immigration. San Francisco: R & E, 1971.

Kim, Richard. The Innocent. Boston: Houghton Mifflin, 1968.

_____. Lost Names; Scenes from a Korean Boyhood. New York: Praeger, 1970.

_____. The Martyred. New York: Braziller, 1964.

Kim, Yong Ik. The Diving Gourd. New York: Alfred Knopf, 1962.

Kimura, Yukiko. "Psychological Aspects of Japanese Immigration," Social Process in Hawaii, VI (1940), 10-20.

Kitagawa, Daisuke. Issei and Nisei: The Internment Years. New York: Seabury Press, 1967.

Kitano, Harry L. Japanese-Americans: Evolution of a Sub-Culture. Englewood Cliffs: Prentice Hall, 1969.

Kitano, Harry H. L. "Japanese American Crime and Delinquency." The Journal of Psychology, LXVI (1967), 253-263.

Knox, George, and Harry Lawton, editors. Analecta: Selected Writings of Sadakichi Hartmann. New York: Herder and Herder, 1970.

Kung, S. W. The Chinese in American Life. Seattle: University of Washington, 1962.

Kurokawa, Minako. Minority Responses. New York: Random House, 1970.

Lang, Olga. Chinese Family and Society. Hamden, Connecticut: Shoe String, 1968.

Lanman, C. The Japanese in America. Tokyo: Japan Advertiser, 1926.

Laviolette, Forrest Emmanuel. Americans of Japanese Ancestry: A Study of Assimilation in the American Community. Toronto: Canadian Institute of International Affairs, 1945.

Lee, Calvin. Chinatown USA. New York: Doubleday, 1965.

Lee, Peter H. Anthology of Korean Poetry. From the Earliest Day to the Present. New York: John Day, 1964.

Lee, Rose Hum. The Chinese in the United States of America. Hong Kong: Hong Kong University, 1960.

_____. "The Decline of Chinatowns in the United States," American Journal of Sociology, LIV (March 1949), 422-432.

_____. "Research on the Chinese Family," American Journal of Sociology, LIV (May 1949), 497-504.

Lee, Virginia. The House That Tai Ming Built. New York: Macmillan, 1963.

Li, Chin-yang. Flower Drum Song. New York: Farrar, 1957.

_____. Lover's Point. New York: Farrar, Straus, 1958.

Li, Tien-yu. Woodrow Wilson's China Policy, 1913-1917. New York: Octagon, 1969.

Lin, Yutang. Between Tears and Laughter. New York: John Day, 1943.

_____. Chinatown Family. New York: John Day, 1948.

_____. The Chinese Theory of Art. New York: Putnam Sons, 1967.

_____. The Chinese Way of Life. New York: World, 1959.

_____. Famous Chinese Short Stories. New York: John Day, 1952.

_____. Miss Tu. London: Heineman, 1950.

_____. Moment in Peking. New York: John Day, 1939.

_____. My Country and My People. Detroit: Gale Research, 1971.

_____. The Vermillion Gate. Westport, Connecticut: Greenwood, 1972.

_____. With Love and Irony. New York: John Day, 1940.

Liu, Jo-yü. The Art of Chinese Poetry. Chicago: University of Chicago, 1970.

Liu, Shih Shun. One Hundred and One Chinese Poems. Hong Kong: Hong Kong University, 1967.

Lowe, Pardee. Father and Glorious Descendant. Boston: Little, Brown, 1943.

Lyman, Stanford M. The Asian in the West. Reno: University of Nevada, 1970.

McClellan, Robert F. The Heathen Chinee. Columbus: Ohio State University, 1971.

McCune, Evelyn B. The Arts of Korea, an Illustrated History. Rutland, Vermont: Charles E. Tuttle, 1962.

McCune, Shannon. Korea: Land of Broken Calm. Princeton: D. Van Nostrand, 1966.

McGraw, John H. The Anti-Chinese Riots of 1885. Seattle: Historical
    Society Publications, Vol. II, Chapter 6.

McKenzie, Roderick Duncan. Oriental Exclusion. San Francisco: R & E, 1970.

McLeod, Alexander. Pigtails and Gold Dust. Caldwell, Idaho: Caxton, 1947.

McWilliams, Carey. Prejudice: Japanese Americans: Symbol of Racial
    Intolerance. Hamden, Connecticut: Shoe String, 1971.

Ma, Wen-huan. American Policy Toward China. New York: Arno, 1970.

Maisel, Albert Q. They All Chose America. New York: Thomas Nelson, 1961.

Masuoka, Jitsuichi, and Preston Valien, editors. Race Relations: Problems
    and Theory. Chapel Hill: University of North Carolina, 1961.

Mears, Eliot Grinnell. Resident Orientals on American Pacific Coast.
    Chicago: University of Chicago, 1925.

Memmi, Albert. The Colonizer and the Colonized. New York: Orion, 1965.

Michener, James. Hawaii. New York: Bantam, 1971.

Miller, Stuart Creighton. The Unwelcome Immigrant. Berkeley: University
    of California, 1969.

Millis, H. A. The Japanese Problem in the United States. New York:
    Macmillan, 1915.

Miner, Earl. The Japanese Tradition in English Literature and American
    Literature . Princeton: Princeton University, 1958.

Misaki, H. K. Delinquency of Japanese in California. Stanford University
    Series in Education-Psychology, vol. 1, 1933.

Mishima, Yukio. The Sound of Waves. (Translated by Meredith Weatherby.)
    New York: Berkeley, 1965.

Mitchison, Lois. The Overseas Chinese. Chester Springs, Pennsylvania:
    Dufour Editions, 1961.

Miyamoto, Kazuo. Hawaii: The End of the Rainbow. Rutland, Vermont: C. E.
    Tuttle, 1964.

Miyoshi, Tami. The Cherry Dance. Los Angeles: Holloway House, 1969.

Moody, John. The Railroad Builders. New Haven: Yale University, 1919.

Mori, Toshio. Yokohama, California. Caldwell, Idaho: Caxton, 1949.

Myer, Dillon Seymour. Uprooted Americans. Tucson: University of Arizona,
    1971.

"New Americans: Where They're Coming From." United States News and World Report, LXX (June 14, 1971), 12-14.

Noguchi, Yone. The Selected Poems of Yone Noguchi. Somerville, Massachusetts: Humphries, Bruce, no date.

Okada, John. No-No-Boy. Rutland, Vermont: Charles E. Tuttle, 1958.

Okimoto, Daniel I. American in Disguise. New York: Walker-Weatherhill, 1971.

Okubo, Mine. Citizen 13660. New York: Columbia University Press, 1946.

Oyanagi, Noble. "The Best Example of Teamwork I Know," English Journal, XXXV (June 1946), 298-299.

Peterson, William. "Success Story: Japanese American Style." The New York Times, January 9, 1966.

Pound, Ezra. Cathay. Princeton: Princeton University, 1965.

_____. The Classic Anthology Defined by Confucius. Cambridge, Massachusetts: Harvard University, 1954.

Ritter, Ed, Helen Ritter, and Stanley Spector. Our Oriental Americans. New York: McGraw-Hill, 1965.

Sandmeyer, Elmer Clarence. Anti-Chinese Movement in California. Urbana: University of Illinois, 1939.

Santos, Bienvenido. You Lovely People. Manila: Benipayo, 1955.

_____. Villa Magdalena. Manila: Erewhon, 1965.

Saxton, Alexander P. The Indispensable Enemy. San Francisco: R & E, 1971.

Seward, George Frederick. Chinese Immigration: Its Social and Economical Aspects. New York: Arno, 1970.

Shen Tso-Chien. What Chinese Exclusion Really Means. New York: Chinese Institute in America, 1942.

Shigetaka, Kaneko. Guide to Japanese Art. Rutland, Vermont: Charles E. Tuttle, 1963.

Smith, Bradford. Americans from Japan. Philadelphia: J. B. Lippincott, 1948.

Smith, W. C. Second Generation Orientals in America. Honolulu: Institute in Pacific Relations, 1927.

Sone, Monica. Nisei Daughter. Boston: Little, Brown, 1953.

Spicer, Edward Holland. Impounded People. Tucson: University of Arizona, 1969.

Stonequist, Everett V. The Marginal Man. New York: Russell and Russell, 1961.

Strong, Edward K. The Second Generation Japanese Problem. New York: Arno, 1970.

Sung, Betty Lee. Mountain of Gold. New York: Macmillan and Co., 1967. Also published as The Story of the Chinese in America. New York: Collier, 1971.

Tachiki, Amy; Eddie Wong; Franklin Odo and Buck Wong, editors. Roots: An Asian American Reader. Los Angeles: University of California, 1971.

Ten Broek, Jacobus, with E. Barnhart and F. Matson. Prejudice, War and the Constitution. Berkeley: University of California, 1954.

Thomas, Dorothy S. The Salvage. Berkeley: University of California, 1952.

_____, and R. Nishimoto. The Spoilage. Berkeley: University of California, 1969.

Tow, Julius Su. The Real Chinese in America. San Francisco: R & E, 1970.

Townsend, Luther Terry. The Chinese Problem. San Francisco: R & E, 1970.

Twain, Mark. Roughing It. New York: Rinehart, 1953.

Viewpoints: Red & Yellow, Black & Brown. Minneapolis: Winston, 1972.

Villa, Jose Garcia. Have Come, Am Here. New York: Viking Press, 1941.

_____. Selected Poems and New. New York: Obolensky Books, 1958.

Wake, Lloyd K. "Shh! An Asian American Speaking," Hokubei Mainichi, February 24, 1970.

Wang, Chi-Chen. Contemporary Chinese Stories. Westport, Connecticut: Greenwood, 1969.

_____. Traditional Chinese Tales. Westport, Connecticut: Greenwood, 1944.

Wolf, Margery. The House of Lim. New York: Appleton-Century-Crofts, 1968.

Wong, Jade Snow. Fifth Chinese Daughter. New York: Harper, 1950.

Wright, Kathleen. The Other Americans. Boston: Lawrence, 1969.

Yamato, Chibashi. Japanese in the United States. Stanford: Stanford Press, 1922.

Young, James Russell. Behind the Rising Sun. New York: Doubleday, Doran, 1941.